The Epistles of John

Westminster Bible Companion

Series Editors

Patrick D. Miller
David L. Bartlett

The Epistles of John

DAVID RENSBERGER

Westminster John Knox Press
LOUISVILLE
LONDON · LEIDEN

Book design by Publishers' WorkGroup
Cover design by Drew Stevens

First edition

Published by Westminster John Knox Press
Louisville, Kentucky

This book is printed on acid-free paper that meets the American National Standards Institute Z39.48 standard. ∞

PRINTED IN THE UNITED STATES OF AMERICA

01 02 03 04 05 06 07 08 09 10 — 10 9 8 7 6 5 4 3 2 1

Library of Congress Cataloging-in-Publication Data

A catalog record for this book is available from the Library of Congress.

ISBN 0-664-25801-8

Contents

Series Foreword

This series of study guides to the Bible is offered to the church and more specifically to the laity. In daily devotions, in church school classes, and in listening to the preached word, individual Christians turn to the Bible for a sustaining word, a challenging word, and a sense of direction. The word that scripture brings may be highly personal as one deals with the demands and surprises, the joys and sorrows, of daily life. It also may have broader dimensions as people wrestle with moral and theological issues that involve us all. In every congregation and denomination, controversies arise that send ministry and laity alike back to the Word of God to find direction for dealing with difficult matters that confront us.

A significant number of lay women and men in the church also find themselves called to the service of teaching. Most of the time they will be teaching the Bible. In many churches, the primary sustained attention to the Bible and the discovery of its riches for our lives have come from the ongoing teaching of the Bible by persons who have not engaged in formal theological education. They have been willing, and often eager, to study the Bible in order to help others drink from its living water.

This volume is part of a series of books, the Westminster Bible Companion, intended to help the laity of the church read the Bible more clearly and intelligently. Whether such reading is for personal direction or for the teaching of others, the reader cannot avoid the difficulties of trying to understand these words from long ago. The scriptures are clear and clearly available to everyone as they call us to faith in the God who is revealed in Jesus Christ and as they offer to every human being the word of salvation. No companion volumes are necessary in order to hear such words truly. Yet every reader of scripture who pauses to ponder and think further about any text has questions that are not immediately answerable simply by reading the text of scripture. Such questions may be about historical and geographical details or about words that are obscure or so loaded with meaning that one cannot tell at a glance what is at stake. They may be about the fundamental meaning of a passage or about what connection a particular text might have to our contemporary world. Or a teacher preparing for a church school class may simply want to know: What should I say about this biblical passage when I have to teach it next Sunday? It is our hope that these volumes, written by teachers and pastors with long experience studying and teaching the Bible in the church, will help members of the church who want and need to study the Bible with their questions.

The New Revised Standard Version of the Bible is the basis for the interpretive comments that each author provides. The NRSV text is presented at the beginning of the discussion so that the reader may have at hand in a single volume both the scripture passage and the exposition of its meaning. In some instances, where inclusion of the entire passage is not necessary for understanding either the text or the interpreter's discussion, the presentation of the NRSV text may be abbreviated. Usually, the whole of the biblical text is given.

We hope this series will serve the community of faith, opening the Word of God to all the people, so that they may be sustained and guided by it.

Introduction

Three small letters toward the back of the New Testament bear the same name as one of the greatest of the New Testament writings, the Gospel of John. Of course, most people are much better acquainted with the Gospel than with these letters. Yet these little documents contain a number of expressions and ideas that most Christians would consider basic to their faith, such as belief in Jesus and the commandment to love one another. Some important items, such as the term *antichrist* and the declaration that "God is love," occur only here in the entire Bible. Despite its small size, even 3 John offers a fascinating glimpse into the mission strategies and internal rivalries of the early church. Indeed, all three of these letters were addressed to quite specific circumstances. In this general Introduction, I will address in broad strokes the circumstances surrounding the letters and the issues involved in them. Each of the three letters also has its own Introduction dealing with its structure and the issues that are special to it.

The "Johannine" Letters

These three letters have a special relationship to the Gospel of John in more than just name. They also share with it a distinctive literary style and way of thinking and speaking about Jesus Christ and the issues of Christian life. For instance, if you compare the story of the Last Supper in John with the version in one of the other Gospels, you will notice that John has entire conversations not found in the others, and that the conversations focus on subjects like Jesus' relation to the Father, his disciples' relation to "the world," their "abiding" in Jesus, their love for one another, and the coming of the Spirit of Truth. These same subjects, presented in an almost identical style of writing, occur in the letters of John as well; and this combination of subject and style does not occur anywhere else in the New Testament.

Because of this unique relationship, the Gospel and letters of John—the "Johannine" writings ("Johannine" being the adjective made from "John")—are generally considered to form a distinct grouping. Their close similarity, and their difference from other New Testament writings, could be caused by a number of possible factors. They could all have the same author; or they could all come from the same time and place; or they could all come from the same Christian community or be addressed to the same circumstances. Indeed, some combination of these possibilities seems likely to be true. I will begin with the question of authorship.

The name "John" attached to all four of these books reflects the fact that early on, by the second century in fact, Christian tradition identified their author as John the son of Zebedee, one of the twelve apostles. It is important to note, however, that no author's name actually appears in the text of any of these writings. The Gospel of John may identify "the disciple whom Jesus loved" (John 13:23; 19:26; 20:2; 21:7, 20, 24) with the composition of the book, while 2 and 3 John speak of their author as "the elder"; but none of these individuals is given a name. How the name "John" got connected with these books is not really known, and it certainly remains possible that the apostle John was associated in some way with the tradition from which all of them ultimately derive. In any case, however, the amount of development in the theology and the historical circumstances suggested by these books makes it unlikely that any of them was written by an apostle. Even the reference in the opening verse of 1 John to "what we have heard, what we have seen with our eyes, what we have looked at and touched with our hands" does not necessarily indicate that the author was an eyewitness of Jesus. The "we" here is rather more that of a group that stretches continuously through time from the appearance of Jesus to the time of the author and his readers, and bears witness to the reality of what was originally seen and heard.

In fact, it is not even certain that the Gospel and letters of John were all written by the same person. Their style and theology are *nearly* identical, but not entirely so. It may seem like nitpicking to point out differences in the use of this or that preposition or turn of phrase as evidence of differences in authorship. Nevertheless, such differences do exist, and it must be added that the author of the letters does not seem to be quite the master of the "Johannine style" that the author of the Gospel is. At quite a number of points in these letters, translators and commentators must wrestle with the difficulties of obscure and ambiguous passages of a sort not found at all in the Gospel of John. There are some theological differences as well. For instance, the letters speak of a direct relationship between Christian believers and God in contexts where the Gospel is more likely to speak of Jesus as mediator between the two. On the whole, there are good reasons to think that "the elder" who wrote the letters may not be the same person as the author of the Fourth Gospel. Indeed, it is not entirely certain that "the elder" wrote 1 John as well as 2 and 3 John, since this title does not occur in the first letter. But there is no adequate evidence to establish a difference between the longer and shorter letters, and it seems best to consider "the elder" as the author of all three.

Who was this "elder" then? Unfortunately, we have no information about him other than what we read in his letters. Even his title is not very helpful. References to "elders" in the early period of Christian history generally are to leadership groups in specific places (see, for example, Acts 14:23; 15:1–6, 22–23; 20:17; 21:18; 1 Tim. 4:14; 5:17–19; Titus 1:5; James 5:14; 1 Peter 5:1–5). Nowhere else do we read of an individual who can be called simply "*the* elder." Perhaps this is simply another unique feature of the Johannine writings and the "brand" of early Christianity that they represent. At any rate, "the elder," as we encounter him in these letters, is a man of authority who speaks of his readers as his "children." He exercises his authority with warmth and carefulness, encouraging and persuading rather than commanding and threatening, even when he has sharp criticisms to make. Moreover, it is clear from all three letters that his authority could be and was challenged, and that he had no real mechanism available to enforce his opinions. (This issue will come up again when I discuss the circumstances of the letters.) Thus, about the most we can say with regard to "the elder" is that he held a respected leadership position within the Christian community addressed by these three letters.

This reminds us that, because of the strong similarity among the Gospel and letters of John and because of some of the specific details they mention, it is common for scholars to think of a distinctive Johannine community, a specific Christian group within which and for which these texts were originally written, whether or not they were all written by the same person. Although this community likely did exist, we don't really know where it was located (though the same tradition that makes the apostle John the author of these books says that he settled in Ephesus). Actually, the references to traveling in 2 and 3 John suggest that the "community" may have been spread out in several nearby cities and towns. It seems likely that this group underwent some development over the course of time.

The issues that are addressed in the Johannine letters are not the same as those in the Fourth Gospel, as will be discussed below. Most scholars believe this indicates that the letters were written later than the Gospel (though a minority opinion suggests that at least some of them were written earlier). Both tradition and scholarship suggest that John was the last of the four New Testament Gospels to be written, coming into being perhaps in the 90s of the first century. The letters, then, would probably date to the period shortly after 100, or even a few years further on in the second century.

Issues in the Johannine Letters

One reason for thinking that the letters are later than the Gospel of John is that they seem to offer commentary on some of its themes and ideas, in a way that suggests that the interpretation of these concepts had become a subject of debate within the community. This is especially true of 1 and 2 John. The Fourth Gospel, for instance, promotes the confession of faith in Jesus as Christ and Son of God (John 20:31), and speaks of his "new commandment" to love one another (John 13:34). First John not only insists on this confession of faith (2:22–23; 4:15), but reflects on its exact nuances and implications (4:2; 5:1, 5) and considers both the newness of the new commandment (2:7–11) and how it relates to faith in Jesus (3:23; 4:7–10, 14–16; see also 2 John 5–7).

It appears, then, that the Johannine letters address issues that have arisen in the community since the writing of the Gospel of John. These issues center on controversies swirling around certain members of the Johannine community, some of whom have actually left it. First and Second John seem to be focused on the same controversy, which will be considered in detail in the Introduction to 1 John. Third John does not make any obvious reference to the issues discussed in the other two letters, and it will be simplest to postpone most of the consideration of 3 John until its own Introduction. In the remainder of this general Introduction, I will look at the major theological issues addressed in the letters, especially 1 and 2 John.

In 1 and 2 John, there are two main themes: belief in Jesus Christ and love for one another. In fact, these two themes are brought into such close relationship with one another that it is impossible to treat them completely separately. First John considers love and belief together as a single, two-sided response to the fact that God sent Jesus into the world as a sacrifice for our sins. This great act of divine love—so great that it moves the elder to declare that God *is* love—calls for a human response that accepts and trusts in its reality (the response of belief) and transforms our own behavior in accordance with the divine pattern (the response of love). We *act out* our belief in our life of love, and our love is *grounded in* what we believe about Jesus. Love is the way people behave when they believe that Jesus is the Messiah, the Christ, the Son of God. By coming into the world as he did, Jesus revealed the essential thing about God—that God is love— and at the same time he revealed that human beings can truly love one another with this same divine love. This is the good news, the gospel message, according to the Johannine letters: God is love, God sent Jesus into the world out of love, and we now have an opportunity to love. For the elder, love is not law, but gospel.

"Believing in Jesus," as these letters understand it, means more than just holding a correct doctrinal position, though it does include correct doctrine. Specifically, the right belief is in "Jesus Christ as having come in flesh" (1 John 4:2; compare 2 John 7). What this rather obscurely worded formulation seems to call for is the acknowledgment that Jesus, the divine Christ and Son of God, entered the world as a physical, mortal human being. Why it was necessary to insist on this will be discussed in the Introduction to1 John, and the full implications will be brought out in the commentary. For now, we may simply note that the Johannine letters want their readers to be absolutely clear that Jesus was not only fully divine, but fully human. For the elder, however, it was not enough simply to believe this claim intellectually. The belief is real only if the believer loves as Jesus loved, loves as God is love. True faith is doing; true action is believing. Real love, divine love, spiritual love arises from the recognition that the divine entered our world as one of us, and it results in down-to-earth, physical acts of caring for other human beings. If Jesus Christ has come in the flesh, then the spiritual and the physical are not in opposition to each other. Physical reality is the place where spiritual reality makes itself known, as love; spiritual reality is what gives physical reality its right orientation, toward love.

If love is the typical and natural expression of Christian faith, then being a Christian obviously requires other people, a community, whom the believer can love. You cannot be a Christian all by yourself. On the other hand, an honest discussion of the Johannine letters (and the Gospel of John, too, for that matter) requires that we notice that the form of their love commandment is "Love *one another.*" This refers to other members of the believing community, not to the world at large, which tends to be considered a hostile place in these writings. Indeed, especially in 2 and 3 John, we sense that love did not always extend even to everyone within the group. The Johannine community, which began its history suffering persecution from outside and went on to experience the ruptures evident in these letters, may have had good reasons for focusing on the sustaining and healing power of love for others within its own body. In stressing mutual love, moreover, this community intended to bear witness to the fact that the Messiah had come, that God had sent a salvation that meant not only personal but social transformation for those who accepted it. Nevertheless, "Love one another" does represent a limitation on love, and it is important to remember that Jesus himself had a more expansive understanding: "Love your neighbor as yourself," he said (Mark 12:28–34, quoting Lev. 19:18), and even, "Love your enemies" (Luke 7:27–36).

While emphasizing the themes of love and belief, the Johannine letters touch on many other issues as well. First John not only declares that God is love, but reminds its readers that this God abides in us and we abide in God. This claim to divine presence is demonstrated by God's gift of the Spirit, and above all by our love for one another, as well as by our belief in Jesus. Yet these letters stress much more clearly than does the Gospel of John that we have this relationship directly with God, now that Jesus has made it possible. Indeed, even the love commandment is seen as a gift directly from God. A reflective reading of these texts, especially 1 John, leaves one with the sense that Christian life is a deeply intimate relationship with a completely loving God.

The question of sin is not ignored, however, particularly by 1 John. Unfortunately, the letter treats this topic in such an obscure, even contradictory, way that the reader is often left baffled as to what is intended. At one point we read that children of God, unlike children of the devil, cannot and do not sin (3:4–10); at another we find comforting assurances of forgiveness if we do sin, and encouragement not to deny our sins (1:5–2:2); at another, both kinds of claims are put side by side (5:16–18). Apparently the author wanted to keep his readers from abandoning the way of love, and so he held out both the reality of a life lived as a child of God (in love that knows no sin) and the reality of divine compassion, so that the readers might not give up when they fell short.

Christians today know Christian communities as churches, often with long-established traditions. Tradition is an important theme in all three Johannine letters, though only 3 John actually uses the word "church." The most common term for the Christian community in these writings, in fact, is "brothers," or, more inclusively and probably more correctly, "brothers and sisters." The use of this expression reflects the ideal of a church where everyone is on the same level. Our author may be "the elder," and may speak of the readers as his "children," but he never forgets that in the end, they are all equally children of one Father, all brothers and sisters. The elder's official title gave him no power to force his will onto others. This represented the continuation of a very ancient kind of structure, or lack of structure, in early Christianity, one where the primary authority, especially for teaching, was the Holy Spirit.

Yet it is clear in these letters that this state of affairs was under stress, and that new relations between tradition and Spirit, and among community members, were being developed. Some people were claiming that the Spirit was leading them in ways contrary to traditional understandings of Jesus and of mutual love. Some people had left the community, or at least the elder's group; some went about teaching unfamiliar doctrines; others refused to accept such traveling messengers and teachers, or at least rejected certain ones. There was conflict, there was confusion, and there were most certainly church politics. It all sounds familiar, perhaps distressingly so. In the midst of these unstable developments, the elder sought to unite tradition and claims to the Spirit around the core of a belief in Jesus Christ, fully human and fully divine, that was expressed as love for one another. Neither tradition as such nor the Spirit as such could be the basic standard for deciding what was true. That standard could only be Jesus Christ, come in the flesh, the revelation of the God who is love; and this standard could ultimately only be applied by the Christian community in whom God was abiding in the Spirit, in belief in Jesus, and in love for one another.

First John

Introduction

I mentioned in the general Introduction to this volume that the Johannine letters seem to offer commentary on some of the themes and ideas of the Gospel of John. This is especially true of 1 John, which in one sense is a kind of a guide to the interpretation of John. But it is by no means a neutral and objective guide, offering scholarly comments on all aspects of the Fourth Gospel. Instead, it is a document forged in controversy and meant to guide its readers away from one kind of interpretation and toward the elder's own position. As with all controversies, certain specific points were at issue, so that 1 John focuses on selected subjects from the Gospel. Moreover, as with all controversies, there was more than one side involved, and the people in the midst of it knew what the parties were talking about even if not every detail was spelled out. We don't have access to what the other parties to this controversy were saying, only to the elder's writing, and a good deal of what he writes only hints at the subjects under dispute. We therefore can only try to deduce what those subjects were from what we find in 1 John; we have no other source of information. There is considerable risk in this type of historical reconstruction, and we need to proceed cautiously. It is not pure guesswork, however, and the process is helpful in trying to understand 1 John.

The Controversy behind 1 John

What makes us think that there *was* a controversy behind 1 John? The evidence of conflict is pretty plain. In 1 John 2:18–27 and 4:1–6, we read of people who "went out from us," whom the author says are "false prophets" who want to deceive the readers; people who are "from the world," not from God; people who are under the influence of the "spirit of error," the "spirit of antichrist"; people who are in fact "antichrists" themselves. These are very strong words, and they suggest that there was indeed a dispute within the community, in the course of which some members, perhaps many, actually left the group. In these passages, the elder makes specific statements about his opponents, the people who "went out from us," and says some other things that may reasonably be thought to refer to them also. Elsewhere in 1 John, we find other remarks that may be added to these to build up a picture of the opponents, even though they are not always specifically mentioned. Using these hints, we can gain some understanding of the nature of the conflict and the issues under dispute.

In the passages just mentioned, the elder expresses concern about people who do not have a proper understanding of Jesus Christ. They "deny that Jesus is the Christ," which seems to mean the same as "denying the Son." They also do not "confess Jesus Christ as having come in flesh." The author speaks of these denials in relation to spirits and discusses whether the spirits come from God or not. Bearing in mind that in the Gospel of John one primary role of the Holy Spirit is guiding believers into new truth (John 14:25–26; 16:12–13), the opponents were probably offering a teaching about Christ that they claimed was given to them under the influence of the Spirit. The exact nature of that teaching, however, is much harder to deduce from the text of 1 John.

The reference to "flesh" in 1 John 4:2 most likely refers to physical, visible human reality, including not only the body but the mortality and various weaknesses that distinguish human life in this world from the immortal life of the spirit. In some way the opponents denied that Christ shared that reality with us; or at least they denied that his humanity was meaningful for the salvation that he brought. This teaching is not very surprising when we realize that in the cultural context of early Christianity, the spirit or mind was often valued much more highly than the flesh or body. We see something similar in 1 Corinthians 15, where Paul has to work mightily to convince his readers that there will be a resurrection of the body, which they might have considered something of a disappointing outlook. Even then, he has to reassure them that this will be a *spiritual* body, a concept that itself could use further explanation. The opponents of 1 John perhaps also hoped for a salvation that would be purely spiritual, an eternal life that would make them not only immortal, but nonphysical as well. For the Savior to give them this life, surely he would have to have overcome all that is physical and limited; he might be the divine Son of God sent from heaven, but he could not really have been mortal, bodily human flesh.

There were Christian groups in the second century and later who actually taught this concept. They were called "docetists," from a Greek word that means "to seem," since their idea was that Christ only *seemed* to be human. The earliest clear references to them are in letters written by Bishop Ignatius of Antioch, in a time and place not far removed from 1 John and its readers. We must be careful to remember, however, that the elder does not provide us with much information about his opponents' teaching, and we cannot be sure that they were full-fledged docetists. Other second-century teachers also made a sharp separation between the Savior's spiritual divinity and his physical humanity, among them the gnostic leader Cerinthus, who, according to legend, was actually opposed by the apostle John. Cerinthus taught that the Christ was a divine being who descended on the human Jesus at his baptism, and departed from him before his crucifixion. This would fit in fairly well with what the elder says about people who "deny that Jesus is the Christ," and with his insistence on believing and confessing that Jesus is the Christ, the Son of God (1 John 3:23; 4:15; 5:1, 5, 10, 13). Again, however, what little we know about 1 John's opponents does not line up completely with what we know about Cerinthus or any other teacher or school of thought. Perhaps the most we can say is that the opponents shared some of the same presuppositions as the docetists and Cerinthus. Certainly we can say that the elder considered their teaching to be a dangerous deception and a manifestation of the dreaded antichrist (on the meaning of this term, see the comments on 1 John 2:18).

How did such a movement arise? We can't really know, although it is possible that it came about as people read the Gospel of John or listened to the traditions behind it in changing circumstances. Perhaps the opponents based their position on Johannine teaching, and yet took it in new directions, following (so they claimed) the leading of the Spirit. That would explain why the elder so often emphasizes that the readers should remain with what they have heard "from the beginning," and why he frequently seems to offer his own interpretations of ideas and expressions from the Fourth Gospel. That Gospel, after all, lays great emphasis on Christ's divinity, on his having "come down from heaven" and being one with God (John 3:13, 31; 6:32–33, 38, 51; 8:23; 10:30; 17:11, 22). By playing up these aspects of John, and perhaps also by taking note of the descent of the Spirit onto Jesus at his baptism and his "giving up the spirit" at his death, the opponents may have developed an understanding of Christ as the divine Son of God who came down from heaven and brought a salvation completely unrelated to the brutal death of the human Jesus.

Whatever the nature and origin of the opponents' teaching, the elder responds by emphasizing the identity of Jesus with the Christ, the Son of

God, precisely in his offering an atoning sacrifice for our sins (1 John 1:7; 2:1–2; 4:10), as the one who came not only with water (perhaps referring to his baptism) but with water and blood (5:6–8). Difficult as it may be to conceive of a Savior who is both fully human and fully divine, 1 John insists that no other conception can reflect the truth and therefore come from the Spirit of truth. The elder also insists that belief in this Savior, divine and human, is inseparable from a life of love for one another. This insistence may imply that the opponents did not regard material acts of mutual love as essential to the Christian life; they are certainly unlikely to have seen the sacrifice of Jesus as a model for their own daily lives. Though 1 John does not directly accuse the "antichrists" of failing to love, there are definite hints in that direction (2:9–11; 3:10–18; 4:8–10, 19–21). In these passages, the author makes a connection between belief that Jesus is the Son of God who suffered a human death for us, and the life of love that takes its inspiration from him. It is likely that the opponents did not make such a connection. Indeed, they may have believed that, having a heaven-sent eternal life of the spirit, they were beyond ethical concerns in general. At any rate, if they believed in some way that they were not capable of sin, some of the elder's puzzling statements on this subject come into clearer focus (1 John 1:5–2:2; 3:4–10; 5:16–18).

The Structure of 1 John

It is also necessary to say something about the way 1 John is put together, its structure—or rather, its lack of structure, for every attempt to provide a comprehensive outline of 1 John ultimately fails. The fact is that 1 John keeps returning to the same subjects over and over again, without seeming to make progress in its argument or to follow an overall plan. It is important to understand this aspect of the character of 1 John in order to keep from getting lost in it, brief though it may be.

To begin with, though we speak of "the first letter of John," 1 John is not actually a letter. Ancient letters used a standard format, which appears quite clearly in 2 and 3 John, but which 1 John does not follow. There is no mention of sender and recipient at the beginning, and no greetings and wishes for well-being at either the beginning or the end. Therefore 1 John is often classified as a sermon or essay; but its lack of a clear outline raises problems for these classifications also. It does seem to fall, in general terms, into the kind of writing that ancient people used to persuade or exhort others to maintain traditional values and to follow certain ethical patterns. Such exhortations often presented models to imitate (1 John uses

Jesus, and even God, as models of love), and reassured the readers that they only needed to be reminded of what they already knew (see 1 John 2:12–14, 21, 27).

Though 1 John seems not to have any clear overall outline, there are several places in it that are quite carefully, even beautifully, structured (for example, 1:5–2:11; and 4:1–18, introduced by 3:23–24). In this book, I have simply treated these and the other units in sequence, without trying to define a comprehensive structure. However, 1 John is not simply thrown together at random either. Its main themes and turns of phrase constantly reappear, in various combinations with one another. At a number of places, it is hard to tell where one unit of thought ends and another begins, since particular sentences seem to function as connections or "hinges" between two units. All this reminds us of our author's fundamental premise that his two main themes, love for one another and belief in Jesus, cannot be kept separate, but, rather, that each leads inevitably to the other. It makes sense, then, for the sections of the text to blend into one another, for ideas and expressions to repeat in a way that provides a kind of network of cross-references throughout the document. It is difficult for the reader to separate off portions of the text for study or to devise a coherent structural outline. But this difficulty only reflects the elder's experience of Christian life as a seamless blend of love and belief, belief and love, with neither one holding sway over the other, and with both making constant reference to one another. The text of 1 John, including its apparent lack of outline, in its own way embodies this experience.

PROLOGUE
1 John 1:1–4

1:1 **We declare to you what was from the beginning, what we have heard, what we have seen with our eyes, what we have looked at and touched with our hands, concerning the word of life—** 2 **this life was revealed, and we have seen it and testify to it, and declare to you the eternal life that was with the Father and was revealed to us—** 3 **we declare to you what we have seen and heard so that you also may have fellowship with us; and truly our fellowship is with the Father and with his Son Jesus Christ.** 4 **We are writing these things so that our joy may be complete.**

I mentioned in the Introduction to 1 John that this text does not begin like a letter. Instead, it rather obviously begins like the Gospel of John. Terms like "the beginning," "the word," "life," "testify," "the Father," and "the

Son" immediately remind the reader of John 1:1–18. This is especially true
for readers who are familiar with John; and the earliest readers of 1 John
almost certainly had this familiarity. The author most likely intended to cre-
ate such a reminder, especially if he was aiming to present a guide to the
interpretation of the Fourth Gospel.

These opening verses, like the opening verses of the Gospel of John,
form a prologue to the text. The purpose of a prologue is to start the
reader thinking about the subject of the text. On opening 1 John, then, one
is immediately drawn into thoughts of "the beginning," of eternity, of the
relationship of the Father and the Son, topics familiar from the Fourth
Gospel. Our author, however, quickly yet subtly leads us to consider these
ideas in a different light. He speaks of "what was *from* the beginning," not
of One who was *in* the beginning. "The beginning," here as elsewhere in
these letters (1 John 2:7, 24; 3:11; 2 John 5–6), seems to refer not to the
beginning of time but to the beginning of the Christian tradition or the
Christian community. The "word of life," moreover, is not a personal
being in whom life was created, but a message that brings life. The elder
does not write that the word was made flesh, but that the life was revealed.
Apparently, it is this revelation that has existed "from the beginning" (of
Christianity), and "we" testify to it; both the revelation and the testimony
are embodied in the "word of life."

The reader familiar with the Gospel of John, then, gets the impression
that the ideas introduced in this prologue are similar to those in the
Gospel, but not identical to them. They seem more oriented toward hand-
ing on a life-giving message, a testimony, than to identifying Jesus Christ
as the eternal Word made flesh. Yet this prologue, like the Gospel's, does
speak of Jesus Christ and makes it clear that it is in him that the revelation
of life takes place. Indeed, the somewhat odd reference to "the eternal life
that was with the Father" undoubtedly refers to Christ as existing before
the creation and as the source of all life (as in John 1:1–4). Of course, we
do not have to keep turning back from 1 John to the Gospel in order to
read and understand it. Yet, as we will see, our understanding of 1 John is
enhanced at many points if we do make some comparison with John.

In the general Introduction, I discussed what is meant by the "we" who
have heard, seen, and touched, and who now testify and declare. The
emphasis on physical perception makes it clear that what was from the
beginning was not simply an abstract message, but something embodied
in a person. Those who witnessed the revelation directly, and those who
stand in continuity with them, attest not only to a theological doctrine or
mystery but to a physical reality. This theme, introduced so vividly here in

the prologue, will be of central importance later in 1 John (especially in chapter 4). Indeed, even the expression "his Son Jesus Christ" is part of this theme (for example, 1 John 3:23; 5:1, 5). Jesus Christ is the Son of God, but he was a human being just the same, bearing the same physical qualities as others. The faith that receives eternal life must be a faith that incorporates this reality.

Such a faith is not something that concerns only the individual believer, however. It is a matter of "fellowship," of community. In this prologue, the author speaks not as "I" but as "we," as one of a group of witnesses reaching back in time to "the beginning" of Christianity. The purpose of their testimony is that others may join in their fellowship, which is not only with one another but with God and with Jesus Christ. "Fellowship" is a term often used in the New Testament to mean sharing or partnership (for example, Gal. 2:9; Phil. 3:10). Here, it suggests that those who are in community with the author and his fellow witnesses to the revelation of life are also in community with God and with God's human Son, in whom that revelation took place. This implies that those who do not share in this community of testimony, that is, those who do not accept the testimony, are missing out on community with God as well.

The outcome of accepting the author's written declaration will be joy, which is not simply happiness or pleasure in the New Testament, but a blessing that comes with the arrival of the Messiah, and thus of God's salvation. The author can only fully rejoice when the readers are part of the community of testimony and belief; and this joy includes the entire witnessing group. Not only do the readers believe as part of a community, rather than simply as individuals, but even the witnesses' fellowship with God is really satisfactory only when the readers are included as well. Relationship with God involves relationship with human beings: this too will be one of the major themes of 1 John. No one can be in fellowship with God, or "abide in God," as the author will say later, without also being in fellowship with other people. For 1 John, the relationship with God that brings eternal life is simply not valid, is really not even possible, without love for one another (3:14, 23–24; 4:7–12). Even those who are most confident of their fellowship with God and with Jesus only find full joy in sharing this fellowship with others.

The prologue of 1 John thus leads the readers from "the beginning," when the life that was with God was revealed in Jesus Christ, through the testimony of those who saw and touched that revelation, down to the readers' own day, when they can join in fellowship with the witnesses, and with God, by accepting the testimony.

WALKING IN THE LIGHT
1 John 1:5–2:11

The chapter and verse divisions in the New Testament books were added long after they were written, and they don't always correspond to the most natural divisions of the text. Following the prologue, for instance, the next natural unit in 1 John is not the rest of chapter 1, but 1:5–2:11. Some interesting patterns can be seen running through this unit. It begins and ends with references to light and darkness, the only uses of these terms in 1 John. It also contains a series of six statements that people might make, most of which the author criticizes. The first three all begin with "if we say" (1:6, 8, 10) and are characterized as lies and deceptions. The other three begin with "whoever says" (2:4, 6, 9), and contain claims that are proved true or false by conduct. Using these two groups of statements, we may divide the unit into two smaller sections, 1:5–2:2 and 2:3–11. (The first words of chapter 2 are really more a parenthetical remark than the beginning of a new unit.) There is thus a great deal of symmetry in the unit; but the symmetry is not perfect (the statements within each of the two groups do not all have the same form). Similarly, while there is often some verbal connection between one statement and the next (especially in the second group), there is no obvious logical progression.

This mixture of careful structuring and imperfect connections is typical of 1 John. The overall theme of the unit is the correspondence that ought to exist between the words and the actions of those who claim to be in relationship with God. It is one thing to claim fellowship with God, as in 1 John 1:3; it is another thing to demonstrate that claim. The claims criticized here might be made by anyone. However, it is quite possible that such statements were actually being made by the author's opponents and that he is already beginning his criticism of them.

God Is Light (1:5–2:2)

1:5 **This is the message we have heard from him and proclaim to you, that God is light and in him there is no darkness at all. ⁶ If we say that we have fellowship with him while we are walking in darkness, we lie and do not do what is true; ⁷ but if we walk in the light as he himself is in the light, we have fellowship with one another, and the blood of Jesus his Son cleanses us from all sin. ⁸ If we say that we have no sin, we deceive ourselves, and the truth is not in us. ⁹ If we confess our sins, he who is faithful and just will forgive us our sins and cleanse us from all unrighteousness. ¹⁰ If we say that we have not sinned, we make him a liar, and his word is not in us.**

2:1 **My little children, I am writing these things to you so that you may not sin. But if anyone does sin, we have an advocate with the Father, Jesus Christ the righteous;** 2 **and he is the atoning sacrifice for our sins, and not for ours only but also for the sins of the whole world.**

First John 1:5 forms a bridge from the prologue to this new unit. It continues the theme of "the message we have heard" (compare v. 3), and it introduces a new theme by asserting that God is light, without any darkness. These are words that need to be carefully understood. Virtually all religious traditions in the ancient world associated God with light. That is why the Gospel of John identifies Jesus with light, in order to promote its claim that Jesus is divine (John 1:4–5; 3:19; 8:12; 9:5; 12:35, 46). The Hebrew Bible, too, associates God with light (for example, Pss. 27:1; 80:1–3, 7, 19; Hab. 3:3–4), though it also associates God with darkness (for example, Exod. 20:21; Ps. 18:9–12; Isa. 50:10–11). Our author shares in the sharp division of the universe into pairs of opposing categories (light and darkness, above and below, etc.) that was common in the religious thought of his day. This way of thinking can be disconcerting to some of us today, since we often think in terms of shades of gray, and we have grown wary of language that associates everything light with goodness and everything dark with badness.

The point that 1 John wants to make, however, is not so much about God's essential nature as it is about God's actions. Several clues point in this direction. "Light" is associated with love in this unit (2:10); and while here the author says that God is light, elsewhere he declares that God is love (4:8, 16). Here, the message once heard is "God is light"; in 3:11, the message is "that we should love one another." By saying that God is light without any darkness, then, the author seems to be saying the same thing as in chapter 4: God is all love. In other words, God's *actions* are characterized entirely by love. The primary implication that the author will draw from this has to do with how people who are in relationship with God should act toward one another.

How is it that this message about God as a God of light and love can be said to be something that "we have heard from him" (which seems to mean "from Jesus")? 1 John does not generally show any interest in the teaching of Jesus, though that teaching certainly does portray God as compassionate and forgiving. Again, we may refer to chapter 4. There we read that God's love was revealed in the sending of Jesus, God's Son, as an atoning sacrifice, so that we might have life (4:9–10). Jesus revealed that God is love by acting out that love in the ultimate way. This is why the author can say here that the message that God is light (equivalent to "God is love") is one that we have heard from him.

Having made this broad thematic statement in verse 5, the author proceeds to draw conclusions from it. As noted above, the first three are expressed in general terms ("If we say . . . ," the "we" now referring to the author and the readers, not the author and other witnesses as in the preceding verses), but they may represent statements of the author's opponents. Those who claim fellowship with the God who is light must obviously walk in the light themselves, that is, they must love one another (2:9–11). (For "walking" as a metaphor for one's way of life, see, for example, Pss. 1:1; 15:2; Rom. 6:4; 8:4; 14:15; for walking in the light of God, or, by contrast, walking in darkness, see Job 29:3; Pss. 56:13; 82:5; Eccl. 2:14; Isa. 2:5; 9:2; Eph. 5:8; Rev. 21:24.) The opponents may have been claiming this fellowship without the corresponding actions (see also the Introduction to 1 John). They, or anyone else acting in such a way, would be lying and not "doing what is true."

This expression (found also at John 3:19–21 in relation to light and darkness) reminds us how important "truth" is in the Gospel and letters of John. "Truth" in these writings means "reality," the reality of God that is revealed in Jesus Christ. However, 1 John in particular is concerned about separating truth from lies and deception within the community by offering specific tests for truth. These tests sometimes have to do with actions (as here and in 2:4; 4:20), and sometimes with belief in Jesus (as in 2:21–22, 26–27; 4:1–6, 5:10). First John does not offer much in the way of compromise and middle-of-the-road moderation. It deals in light and darkness, truth and falsehood, love and hate. Yet however much the author may be concerned for defining who remains in "fellowship" with God and with the community, he himself never advocates hatred. Rather, in his view, it is those who break fellowship with the community and its message about Jesus and its love for one another who engage in deception and hatred.

The light, love, and truth that are characteristic of God become models for us to imitate in verses 6–7. Those who act in accordance with truth are those who walk in the light of love, as God is in this light (an easier concept than "God *is* light" to relate to human actions). As we will see, the imitation of God will become a central ethical theme in 1 John. It suggests that the essential characteristic of God's actions, love, is available to those who have accepted the revelation in Jesus Christ as a model for their own actions. It also suggests that they are expected to take up this model and follow it in concrete ways.

The imitation of God, as 1 John expounds it, does not mean that people are expected to exercise divine knowledge or power, nor does it mean that they can claim to live in sinless perfection. Indeed, precisely this claim is what the author now proceeds to reject in 1:8–2:2 (these claims differ from the others in 1:5–2:11 in that they are impossible to enact in themselves, rather than being inconsistent with certain other actions). It may be that some in the author's community were actually claiming that their relationship with God and with Jesus had made them incapable of sin, or at least shielded them from the guilt of sin ("we have no sin"), no matter what they did. It seems self-evident to most of us that no human being can make such a claim, for it flies in the face both of common experience and of a widespread biblical conviction (1 Kings 8:46; Pss. 14; 143:2; Eccl. 7:20; Mark 10:18; Rom. 3:9–26). The difficulty, however, is that the author himself makes exactly this claim in 3:4–10: those who have been born of God do not sin! (See also 5:16–18.) Indeed, already in this section, the author, having just said that those who claim not to sin do not have the truth in them, goes on to say the same thing about those who do sin by disobeying God's commandments (2:4).

I will address this awkward contradiction further in commenting on chapter 3. Here it may be enough to point out the author's purpose in writing expressed in 2:1: that the readers may not sin. Therefore he holds up the ideal of genuine ethical transformation, of walking in the light, of being children of God who do not sin. But he also offers the comforting assurance that when we do sin, as we inevitably will, it is not the end of our relationship with God. Rather than living in a state of denial about our sin, we must acknowledge it, in the confidence of God's forgiveness and cleansing. In order to have the truth, we must both recognize our distance from God and commit ourselves to God's ways. First John does not use the language of spiritual and moral growth, which might be more familiar to us. Instead, it presents the difficult (but not unrealistic) paradox that God's people cannot truthfully claim either to be without sin, or to know God when they ignore God's will.

The acknowledgment of sin is called "confession." Confession of sin, for most of us, means either a generic confession in the context of public worship, or a specific but private confession to God, to a cleric, or to the person we have offended. In the New Testament, however, confession of sin is generally both public and specific (Mark 1:5; Acts 19:18; James 5:16). Our author may have this in mind as well, especially since he speaks of confessing "sins," not "sin" in the abstract. Most of us would find such an open confession of specific sins to be an act requiring extraordinary courage and humility. Generally, only the most radical sects or the most dire circumstances in Christian history have demanded it. The language here reminds us that many of the New Testament texts were written in just such radical and acute circumstances. In the polite and often impersonal atmosphere of many modern churches, we are seldom inclined to acknowledge anything specific about our lives, least of all our sins. Perhaps real "fellowship with one another" implies something radically different, a level of intimacy that would let us abandon what amounts to a claim—in public—that "we have not sinned," and open ourselves to our brothers and sisters as we do to God.

Such an intimacy could only be possible where people really believe that God is "faithful and just" (or "righteous") enough to forgive those who confess. Much of the language of assurance in 1 John 1:7–2:2 is drawn not so much from the traditions peculiar to the Gospel and letters of John as from the wider traditions of early Christianity, especially those associated with Paul. Like Paul, our author relates God's righteousness to forgiveness rather than punishment; and he encourages the reader by appealing to the faithfulness of God (1 Cor. 1:9; 10:13; 1 Thess. 5:24; see also, for example, Heb. 10:23). Though the individual themes of redemption in Jesus' blood, forgiveness of sin, and cleansing are fairly common in the New Testament, we find them in combination, as here, only in a limited number of texts; but these are spread broadly across the New Testament canon (Matt. 26:28; Eph. 1:7; Heb. 9:12–14; Rev. 1:5). The idea that Jesus' death was an "atoning sacrifice" is actually rather rare in the New Testament (see 1 John 4:10; Heb. 2:17). But we do read that God is righteous, and justifies believers through the atoning sacrifice of Jesus' blood, in Romans 3:21–26. "Atonement" (which means "expiation" [of sins] rather than "propitiation" [of God]) alludes to the Day of Atonement ritual, which also links blood, cleansing, and atonement (see Leviticus 16).

Thus our author is appealing to concepts of God's forgiveness of sins through the sacrifice of Jesus that were widely held in the early church, in order to encourage his readers not to deny their misdeeds, but to confess them and allow the light of God's love to shine on them for healing and for cleansing. To deny that we have sinned is to make even God a liar, because abandoning the truth of our nature also deprives us of the truth of God's nature as loving and forgiving. If we are to have God's truth in us, then we must also have our own truth, even if it is not always a pretty picture. As in Paul's letters, the righteousness or justice of God is not a terrifying thought for sinners, but a comforting one (see also 1 John 3:19–20). God is "faithful and just," which might be paraphrased, "God may be trusted to do what is right." And what is right is the loving forgiveness of those who turn to God in honest confession.

One term in this passage deserves a moment's special attention. The word translated "advocate" in 2:1 is the same word (sometimes translated "comforter" or "counselor") that is applied to the Holy Spirit in the Gospel of John (14:16–17, 26; 15:26; 16:7–11). It is not used anywhere else in the New Testament. The meaning here is somewhat different from that in the Gospel, and seems closer to the Greek word's ordinary sense of "sponsor" or "patron," someone who could win favor for a person in an official setting. Ancient Jewish belief, beginning already in the Hebrew Bible, knew of heavenly figures who could intercede for the suffering people of God or for people who are falsely accused (Job 16:19–21; 33:23–26; Zech. 1:12–13). It also spoke of earthly advocates who intercede with God for sinners (Gen. 20:7; Exod. 32:11–14, 30–32; 1 Sam. 12:19–25; Job 42:8–10). Early Christians seem to have combined these two kinds of figure as one way of understanding the role of Jesus, seeing him as the advocate in heaven interceding for sinners (Rom. 8:34). Our author also pictures Jesus in this way. Indeed, his thinking resembles that of the letter to the Hebrews in understanding Jesus both as heavenly intercessor and as the sacrifice offered for sins (Heb. 7:23–27). Like Paul and the author of Hebrews, he uses this image of Jesus to offer encouragement to believers about their standing before God. In fact, though elsewhere 1 John seems hostile to "the world" (for example, in 2:15–17), here the author speaks of Jesus' sacrifice as being offered not only for believers' sins, but for those of the whole world. This suggests that even for 1 John the possibility of a mission to bring the world to belief remains open; or perhaps even (though this seems less likely) that the author understands Jesus as intercessor for all of sinful humanity, believers and unbelievers alike.

Obeying the Commandment (2:3–11)

2:3 **Now by this we may be sure that we know him, if we obey his commandments. ⁴ Whoever says, "I have come to know him," but does not obey his commandments, is a liar, and in such a person the truth does not exist; ⁵ but whoever obeys his word, truly in this person the love of God has reached perfection. By this we may be sure that we are in him: ⁶ whoever says, "I abide in him," ought to walk just as he walked.**

⁷ Beloved, I am writing you no new commandment, but an old commandment that you have had from the beginning; the old commandment is the word that you have heard. ⁸ Yet I am writing you a new commandment that is true in him and in you, because the darkness is passing away and the true light is

already shining. ⁹ Whoever says, "I am in the light," while hating a brother or sister, is still in the darkness. ¹⁰ Whoever loves a brother or sister lives in the light, and in such a person there is no cause for stumbling. ¹¹ But whoever hates another believer is in the darkness, walks in the darkness, and does not know the way to go, because the darkness has brought on blindness.

Although this passage rather suddenly changes the subject to "knowing him," it does continue both the theme of truth and lying and the format of examining claims that are not matched by conduct. Indeed, the end of the section brings us around again to the beginning in 1:5: no one can truly claim to be in the light of God if they are walking in the darkness of hatred. As before, this author's way of thinking knows no middle ground. There is no gray area, no benign indifference. There is only light or darkness, love or hatred. We may find this absolutism discomforting; but it at least has the virtue of putting the issues in the most basic and starkest possible terms.

The idea here is a very straightforward one, that a claim to relationship with God should be verified by a life lived in the way that God desires. However, a number of the details of the way in which this idea is expressed are unclear or ambiguous (though English translations do not always display these ambiguities). It may be best to treat these first, then consider the sense of the whole passage.

Who is it whose commandments must be kept by those who claim to know him? Reading directly from the preceding passage, one would suppose that it is Jesus (2:1). But there is a slight break in thought between verses 2 and 3, and the subject may have changed. Moreover, 1 John almost always speaks of "knowing" God, rather than Jesus, and always speaks of God, not Jesus, as the giver of commandments (1 John 3:22–24; 4:21; 5:2–3; note also 2 John 4–6). Most likely, then, the reference is to God. Yet when the author speaks of "walking just as he walked" in verse 6, the reference must surely be to Jesus (and in fact a different Greek pronoun is used in "he walked"). This requires an abrupt transition from "I abide in him" (meaning God) to "walk just as he walked" (meaning Jesus) in verse 6. But many of the statements in this passage may have been formulas that were well known to the readers, who could therefore sort out the pronouns more easily than we can.

Verse 5 contains several difficulties. It may not be obvious at first, but the phrase "the love of God" is ambiguous, in English as in Greek: it could mean "our love for God," or it could mean "God's love for us." This unclarity occurs several times in 1 John (and elsewhere in the New Testament). Here, the reference is probably to our love for God (compare 5:3), which would be a more natural parallel to our knowledge of God and our abiding in God, of which this passage also speaks. We might also wonder what it means to say that our love for God "reaches perfection." The idea is that love reaches *completion*, achieves its intended goal (compare 4:12). Finally, the NRSV, like many other translations, places a period in the middle of verse 5, after "perfection," so that "by this" leads into verse 6. However, the earliest Greek manuscripts had no punctuation at all, and it is at least as likely that the major break belongs at the end of verse 5, and that "by this" refers backward to obeying God's word.

The difficulties in verses 7–8 are more obvious, as the writer plays with the conception of "new" and "old" commandments. The commandment in question, of course, is the love commandment, though this is not spelled out until verses 9–11. But how can it be both an old and a new commandment? It is old because it is familiar from the Christian tradition known to the readers (as found in John 13:34–35; 15:12, 17). It is what they "have had from the beginning," that is, "the message you have heard from the beginning" (1 John 3:11). On the other hand, it is a "new" commandment, in part because it is called that in John 13:34. But what really makes it new, both in John and in 1 John, is that it belongs to the new era brought in by the coming of the Messiah Jesus, a new era that is now dawning and pushing back the darkness of the former age.

I will return to this theme a bit later. First we must deal with one last obscurity in the text. According to the NRSV and many other translations, it is the new commandment "that is true in him and in you" (v. 8). But this does not reflect the grammar of the Greek, where the pronoun rendered "that" has a form that cannot refer to "commandment." A more accurate translation would be, "Yet I am writing you a new commandment, [namely] *that which* is true in him and in you." It is not simply that the commandment is true, but that the commandment *consists of* what is true, in Jesus and in the readers. In the language of the Gospel and letters of John, the thing that is true in Jesus would be the divine truth, the divine reality, that he brought into the world and made known. By identifying the new commandment with "what is true in him and in you," the author *identifies the revelation made in and by Jesus Christ with the commandment to love one another*, and says that this truth is also being demonstrated by the Christian readers.

These grammatical details may seem like trivia, but they can be significant for understanding the overall thrust of the passage. First John, unfortunately, tends toward this kind of obscurity; often enough, the first task in reading it is trying to figure out what exactly the author was trying to say! Once we have done this, we can go on to ask about his meaning.

The passage is about knowing God and abiding in God. It makes the general point that people who claim to have such a relationship with God ought to conduct themselves in accordance with God's will. This is an obvious enough proposition; but the author goes on to claim more specifically that God's will can be seen in the way that "he walked," that is, in the life of Jesus, and more specifically still in the commandment of love that Jesus gave. For 1 John, any claim to intimate relationship with God that is not accompanied by the love for other people that Jesus both commanded and exemplified is simply a lie.

To know God, to love God, to abide in God: these are the terms of relationship that 1 John emphasizes. Knowing God, in biblical terminology, means having a direct, personal, and indeed intimate acquaintance with God. On the one hand, it is as basic and simple as knowing a friend, a husband, a mother. On the other hand, it is beyond any knowledge of that sort, because the One who is known is the Creator who existed before all things, and exists in an endless depth of being. We cannot fully penetrate that depth; and yet, we can know God. Indeed, the prophets of the Hebrew Bible speak of a time to come when the people's knowledge of God will be complete (Jer. 31:31–34; Hos. 6:1–3; Hab. 2:14). That ultimate knowledge is what Paul means when he says, "Now I know only in part; then I will know fully, even as I have been fully known" (1 Cor. 13:12).

Like Jeremiah, the prophet Ezekiel also promised a new covenant, but instead of knowledge of God, he spoke of God dwelling among the people, the Spirit of God inhabiting them (Ezek. 36:26–27; 37:26–28). The language of "abiding" in God and God abiding in us that we find in the Gospel and letters of John may reflect a sense of the fulfillment of this promise. (In the Gospel, Jesus always stands between the believers and God in this relationship; 1 John, by contrast, often speaks of a direct relationship of abiding between Christians and God [2:5–6; 3:24; 4:12–16].) This language, which is virtually unique in ancient religion, implies the strongest sense of oneness with God, even while maintaining a distinction of identity. Our author's concern, however, is not with describing this relationship, but with discerning its reality.

No one can completely know God in this life; yet 1 John says that our love of God can be complete, can be perfected, if we obey God's word, God's commandment—meaning the commandment of love. To love God means to obey God; and to obey God means to love one another. Our claim to love God becomes fully real only when we love one another (4:20). For the prophets also, the knowledge of God had an ethical component (Jer. 9:6, 23–24; Hos. 4:1–2). At the end of 1 John, we read that "the Son of God has come and has given us understanding so that we may know him who is true," that is, the true God. By offering himself in the ultimate act of love, Jesus made known the God who is love (4:7–10); the truth revealed in Jesus is the commandment to love one another (2:8; 3:11). Therefore, our knowledge of God must be grounded and demonstrated in love for our brothers and sisters. The author of 1 John gives neither a detailed ethical code nor a set of basic principles from which such a code could be derived. All the ethics we need, he seems to say, is "Love one another." Whatever is in accordance with this is the fulfillment of God's commandment, and validates our knowledge of God, our love of God, our abiding in God. If this seems too easy or simplistic, 1 John 3:16–17 gives us an impression of its real depths.

"Whoever loves a brother or sister lives in the light," according to 2:10. At the risk of sounding like the lawyer who asked Jesus a similar question (Luke 10:29), we do need to inquire how broadly the term "brother or sister" is meant to extend here. Though Jesus' answer to that question was as broad as possible—indeed, he stretched love to include even our enemies (Luke 6:27–36)—in the love commandment of the Gospel of John we find it to be more restricted: "Love *one another*" (John 13:34–35; 15:12, 17). It seems clear that this refers specifically to fellow-disciples, fellow-believers; and the same range is evident in 1 John as well (see 3:11, 14, 23; 4:7–12; also 2 John 5). Such a focus on love within the community is often found in small, socially isolated religious groups, as is the hostility toward the outside world that we will find in the very next passage of 1 John (the Essene writers of the Dead Sea Scrolls furnish another example from antiquity). It is somewhat dismaying to think of Christian love as limited in this way. On the other hand, when we reflect on the amount of blood that Christians have shed (and still do shed) among one another, perhaps 1 John can remind us that while we may want to love the whole wide world, we should not skip over our nearer brothers and sisters on the way there.

The Jews who were Jesus' followers and laid the foundations for Christianity, like many of their fellow-Jews, looked forward eagerly to a time when God would establish a new creation, a new age of peace and justice; when God's people would live free from foreign oppression, and would know God and obey God perfectly; when the Spirit of God would be poured out on them all; and when God's servants who had died would be restored to an everlasting life. These hopes were based on texts from the prophets of the Hebrew Scriptures, including Isaiah 11 and the passages noted above. The early Christian claim that Jesus was the Messiah ("Christ" in Greek), that he had been raised from the dead, and that those who believed in him were filled with the Holy Spirit was essentially a claim that this messianic age has arrived. That claim became problematic when it became clear that injustice, sin, and death had not been done away with. Yet Christian teachers insisted that "the darkness is passing away and the true light is already shining," as 1 John 2:8 puts it, and that believers had access to the power and the way of life that are characteristic of this new era. The designation of the commandment to love one another as a "new commandment" in the Gospel of John and in 1 John corresponds to this belief. Even though it was by now an "old commandment," its messianic freshness remained. (Note that in 2:8 the author does not speak of what *was* true in Jesus, but of what *is* true.) If Christians claim that Jesus is the Messiah, the Son of God (John 20:31), then they are both enabled and obliged to live as if it is true, as if the messianic age of righteousness and obedience to God, the new creation, has dawned. Precisely within the Christian community, among "brothers and sisters," they must live the new life, the messianic life, the life of mutual love.

Their empowerment and their obligation are made all the stronger by the fact that the Messiah himself showed the way of love in his own life, and especially in laying down his life for those whom he loved (John 13:1; 15:12–14). To abide in God, to walk in the light of this new age, they must walk as he walked. The imitation of Christ thus becomes central to 1 John's ethic of love. As elsewhere in the New Testament, this imitation does not focus on the details of Jesus' lifestyle, nor does it seek to make the disciple his equal through moral effort. Rather, it focuses on his self-giving love (for example, Rom. 15:1–7; Eph. 4:32–5:2; Heb. 13:11–16; 1 Peter 2:21–25). Love is the way to "walk just as he walked," to walk in the light as God is in the light.

First John's concern for validating claims to know, love, and abide in God by how people live is one that has been expressed by many Christian teachers in many times and places. This author, however, had a particular reason to express it in the circumstances of his community, which he saw as being threatened by opponents from within. "By this we may be sure" in 2:3 and 5 is one of many phrases throughout 1 John that indicate his interest in criteria for discerning what is true and genuine in claims to relationship with God. We will encounter it (and other expressions, such as "by this we know") frequently in chapters 3 and 4. The author's primary concern throughout is to enable his community to know what truly characterizes the relationship with God that spells eternal life. By setting forth such criteria, he can assure the readers that their experience is valid (assuming that it is in accordance with the criteria!), and at the same time undercut the opponents, whom he considers to have failed these tests. The opponents claim to know, love, and abide in God; but they fail to love their brothers and sisters (see the remarks on 1 John 3:11–17). Part of their failing, as we will see later, is that they do not recognize the saving value of Jesus' human, physical life and death, and therefore also see no value in imitating his example of sacrificial love. Because of all this, they abide, not in the light of God, but in the darkness of the old world that is passing away; not in eternal life, but in death.

This may remind us that, just as love for God must be seen in concrete love for other people, abstract theological discussions come out of real-life circumstances and conflicts. Other times, including our own time, may bring forth similar circumstances. Our author's opponents are long gone; but their ideas and his arguments against them have resurfaced in many ways in Christian history. There are always some who offer ways of knowing God and understanding Jesus that do not involve mutual love. It may be a matter of spiritual laws or doctrinal codes, traditional values or a new spirituality. Whatever it may be, the author of 1 John would have us know that if it is not about love for one another, it is not about the God of Jesus Christ.

CHILDREN, FATHERS, YOUNG PEOPLE
1 John 2:12–14

2:12 I am writing to you, little children,
   because your sins are forgiven on account of his name.
13 I am writing to you, fathers,
   because you know him who is from the beginning.
I am writing to you, young people,
   because you have conquered the evil one.
14 I write to you, children,
   because you know the Father.
I write to you, fathers,
   because you know him who is from the beginning.
I write to you, young people,
   because you are strong
   and the word of God abides in you,
   and you have overcome the evil one.

This little section carries on the themes of forgiveness of sins and knowing God from the preceding section. It also gives reasons for the author's writing, which expand on the purpose stated in 2:1. Beyond this, however, the passage has no obvious logical connection with what comes before or after it. Indeed, the sudden way in which "his name" is introduced in verse 12 may suggest that the whole passage is largely built up from slogans that were well known to the readers. On the other hand, it is in itself the most carefully structured unit in 1 John. It consists of two sets of three statements (the first comprising vv. 12–13, and the second v. 14), each statement containing the verb "write," followed by "to you," the name of a group, and an observation about the group.

The relations among the various statements are quite complex. The first question is, to whom do the group designations refer? "Children" or "little children" is the author's way of addressing the entire body of readers (several times in chapter 2, as well as 3:7, 18; 4:4; 5:21). It is a common way for a teacher to address pupils, and is not meant to be condescending (except to the extent that the teacher-pupil relationship overall involved some measure of condescension in that culture). At any rate, "(little) children" does not refer to a literal age group. The same is likely true, then, of "fathers" and "young people." This author desires that all believers, not only limited circles, have such qualities as knowing God and possessing God's word within. The naming of different age-related groups is simply a figure of speech to encompass an entire people, both old and young, a figure that is found fairly often in the Bible (for instance, in Exod. 10:9; Psalm 148:12; Jer. 31:13; Ezek. 9:6). It is somewhat less certain whether these terms are also meant to include both genders ("young people" [NRSV] is literally "young men"). That is possible. However, while women play prominent parts in the Gospel of John (4:4–42; 11:20–27; 20:11–18), the language here may indicate that in later times their role in the community was reduced.

On the whole, though, we may take it that the statements in this passage are meant to refer to the Christian readers in general. The statements themselves interweave in an intricate manner. On the one hand, it is obvious that the remark addressed to the children in verse 14 is very similar to both remarks to the fathers. Likewise, the remark to the little children in verse 12 can be seen as related to both remarks to the young people (since the "evil one" is related to sin). On the other hand, the statement at the beginning of each group, addressed to the children, is further explained in the two statements that follow, addressed to the fathers and young people. Forgiveness of sins means the defeat of the evil one, which is accomplished by the one whom the fathers know. Knowing God means knowing Jesus and having God's word within. Thus two themes, knowing God and Jesus and conquering sin and the devil, are brought into close relationship by this complex pattern of repetition and variation. The use of such patterns was considered a means of enlivening and refining one's writing in ancient times.

Several specific expressions in this passage still need some consideration. Because "from the beginning" elsewhere in 1 John refers to the beginning of Christian tradition (1:1; 2:7, 24; 3:11; the exception is 3:8), "him who is from the beginning" probably refers to Jesus. Of course, since knowing Jesus is *the* means of knowing God in the Gospel and letters of John (see especially John 14:6–10), the "children" who know the Father and the "fathers" who know the one who is from the beginning have essentially the same knowledge. The evidence of this knowledge, the author has just finished saying, is keeping the commandment to love one another, the word of God that abides within (2:3–11; see also 4:7–8).

Cleansing and forgiveness of sins were related to Jesus' atoning sacrifice in the preceding passage. Here they come through his name (compare Luke 24:47; Acts 10:43; in Acts 2:38 and 22:16 this connection is made with reference to baptism). In ancient thought, a person's name encompassed his or her entire identity. Our author later refers to Jesus' name as the object of Christian belief (3:23; 5:13), very much in line with the usage of the Gospel of John (1:12; 2:23; 3:18). The meaning of this is seen in John 20:31: "These are written so that you may come to believe that Jesus is the Messiah, the Son of God, and that through believing you may have life in his name." The name of Jesus encompasses his identity as Messiah and Son of God, an identity that makes him the bringer of eternal life into the world. Believing in his name means acknowledging this identity, and so receiving life and forgiveness. Those who hold this belief are also able to conquer the world (1 John 5:4–5), since it was Jesus who originally made this conquest (John 16:33). "Conquering" the evil one is virtually the same thing ("overcome" in v. 14 translates the same Greek word), since the world is ruled by the evil one (1 John 5:19; John 12:31; 14:30; 16:11; 17:15). (The devil is also called "the evil one" in 1 John 3:12; 5:18–19; but the term is rare in the New Testament and other ancient literature, except, for some reason, in the Gospel of Matthew.)

Having expressed his *purposes* for writing in 1:4 and 2:1 (see also 5:13), the author here lays out several *reasons* for doing so. As in 2:21, he says that he writes, not because he thinks the readers are weak or ignorant, but in order to build on their strengths. (Paul does something similar in 1 Thess.

4:1, 9–10; 5:1–2.) The readers are strong; they know God and Jesus; through Jesus, their sins are forgiven and they have overcome the evil one. After the set of warnings in 1:5–2:11, the author reassures the readers that he does not think they are likely to fall into those traps. Such combinations of warning and reassurance were common in the ancient rhetoric of encouragement and exhortation, and they are not uncommon in sermons throughout Christian history, down to this day. This passage serves to remind the reader of the gifts and resources that God has made available. Whatever the pitfalls in the Christian life, the fundamental fact of salvation remains, and our relationship with God and the strength God gives us are there to sustain us and keep us from losing heart, or losing our way. With these words of encouragement, the author helps the readers to feel that they are on his side, and to read the cautions and warnings that follow with a sense of confidence rather than apprehension.

DO NOT LOVE THE WORLD
1 John 2:15–17

2:15 **Do not love the world or the things in the world. The love of the Father is not in those who love the world;** [16] **for all that is in the world—the desire of the flesh, the desire of the eyes, the pride in riches—comes not from the Father but from the world.** [17] **And the world and its desire are passing away, but those who do the will of God live forever.**

After the tightly organized message of encouragement in 2:12–14, the reader next encounters this much more loosely structured warning. The Christian readers may have conquered the evil one, but they still need to be admonished about the seduction of the world that is ruled by the evil one (1 John 5:19). It is not a harsh admonition, but it reminds us once again of 1 John's way of seeing everything in terms of stark oppositions: one can love God or one can love the world; but no one can love both. The reasons for this are spelled out in terms of absolute contrast between God and the world, with no room allowed for middle ground.

The contrast between God and the world in 1 John may be the sharpest in the entire New Testament. As in the Gospel of John, 1 John can present the world both as the object of God's love and salvation (1 John 2:2; 4:9, 14; see John 3:16–17; 6:33, 51; 12:46–47), and as fundamentally opposed to God and to the Christ sent to save it, and to those who believe in him (1 John 3:1, 13; 4:4–5; 5:4–5, 19; in the Gospel of John, see, for example, 8:23; 15:18–19; 16:8–11, 33; 17:9–16, 25). This understanding of the world reflects a distinct set of ideas: that God created the world and sent Christ to save the *human* world specifically; but that the human world rejected him as its redeemer. It is the human world—not the natural creation as such—that is understood as maintaining an organized opposition to God, one that results in hatred and oppression among human beings. Much of this is simply presupposed in 1 John, rather than being set out as thoroughly as it is in the Fourth Gospel. From the texts in 1 John alone it would be easy to get the impression that the created world in its essence is opposed to God, an idea closer to the thinking of ancient gnosticism.

It is not simply "the world"—the whole human system opposed to God—that the readers are warned not to love, but "the things in the world." Before we can jump to the conclusion that this refers to the created objects in the world as such, the author specifies what he means by "all that is in the world." The three phrases that he uses to do this are not as clear as we might wish; but they all speak of "desire" or "pride," that is, of human *responses* to things in the world, not of the things themselves. We are warned against loving, not the created objects, but our own desire for them. This desire and pride do not come from God, the Creator of the objects, but from the world, the human system of self-centeredness that always seeks its own gratification rather than the glory of its Creator. In the words of Thomas Merton, "Instead of worshipping God through His creation we are always trying to worship ourselves by means of creatures."

This seems to be the general sense of the passage; but we can be more specific about the three phrases in verse 16. They speak of desire or pride that *derives from* the flesh, the eyes, and riches, respectively. "The desire of the flesh" does not mean desire *for* the flesh, but desire that *originates in* the flesh. The latter term *flesh* can also have a variety of meanings. It can mean the human body, but that is not really its sense here; nor does it refer specifically to sexuality in this context. Unlike other passages in the Gospel and letters of John, it also does not mean human nature as such, in contrast to the divine (compare 1 John 4:2 and 2 John 7). Rather, as in many other New Testament contexts, it means something similar to "the world," although on a more individual level rather than a universal one. It means the force in human nature that drives us to center on ourselves and our own wants, rather than on the needs of others or the will of God. We find similar references to the "desires of the flesh" in Galatians 5:16, 24; Ephesians 2:3; 1 Peter 2:11 (similarly, "worldly passions" in Titus 2:12), and in other ancient moral writers, Christian, Jewish, and pagan. "The desire of the eyes" is a more difficult expression, not really paralleled anywhere else. Perhaps it means desire as stimulated by the senses, in contrast to desire originating inwardly ("the flesh"). "The pride in riches" is clearer. The word translated "riches" (originally meaning "life," and then "means of living"; a different word is used for eternal life) also occurs in 3:17, where the NRSV renders it "goods." The danger here is no doubt also the same as it is there, that material possessions loom so large for us that they make us arrogant (whether we feel arrogant or not!) and cut us off from people in need.

Unlike the other New Testament passages noted above, 1 John does not speak of multiple "desires" but of "desire" itself. The thought is similar to James 4:1–4. The self-centered desire that "comes not from the Father" makes us friends with the world, which in this sense means friends only of ourselves. We want what we want: this slogan is used to sell us cars, clothes, food, and appliances. It works very well, too, because the culture of the "developed nations" today has no sense of anything that ought to restrain or oppose personal and corporate desire. "I want it" is considered an automatic justification for anything we acquire (sometimes dressed up as "I deserve it," which may or may not be true). Hence we have an entire industry (television) that exists for no other reason than to increase "the desire of the eyes." Jesus' teaching that "You cannot serve God and mammon" (Matt. 6:24) is likely to be met with a blank stare from those who have never heard that there is any God *but* mammon. Speaking the Christian message of self-giving rather than self-enhancement, of love rather than desire, of God rather than ourselves, has become like whistling into a very loud wind, a hurricane of advertising, entertainment, and political marketing. Who will hear it? How can we shout it loudly enough? We get some unwanted help from ecological disasters, which suggest that the created world will not bear what the human world wants to load onto it. But in the end the message can best be promoted by putting it into action in our own lives—which is what 1 John calls for. Perhaps the church needs more Amish and fewer marketeers.

The either-or choice of values that 1 John offers us is expressed most sharply by the question, "Whom do you love?" Or, as Jesus phrased it, "Where your treasure is, there your heart will be also" (Matt. 6:21). If those who love the world do not have the love of God in themselves, this need not mean that they are blasphemers or blatantly hostile to religion. Our author insists that the love of God cannot be separated from love for our brothers and sisters (2:5–6, 9–11; 3:16–17; 4:7–21). Those who love the world, that is, who love their own desires, lose sight of a love that extends beyond themselves, reaching up to the God who made and redeemed them and out to the other people who need them. The teaching of our culture is, "If only I had that, I would be what I long to be." The teaching of 1 John, of Jesus, of Paul, and of a multitude of heroes and heroines of the Christian faith, is, "If only I gave that away, I would be what I was made to be." For "the world and its desire are passing away" (2:17). They have no permanence, despite their evident solidity. It is not so much that they are transient by nature as that they belong to the "darkness," to the lack of love that is also passing away as the light of the new era brought in by Jesus Christ prevails (2:8). What will last is what is in accord with the will of God; and that will, as 1 John never tires of saying, is love.

THE COMING OF THE ANTICHRIST
1 John 2:18–27

2:18 **Children, it is the last hour! As you have heard that antichrist is coming, so now many antichrists have come. From this we know that it is the last hour.** [19] **They went out from us, but they did not belong to us; for if they had belonged to us, they would have remained with us. But by going out they made it plain that none of them belongs to us.** [20] **But you have been anointed by the Holy One, and all of you have knowledge.** [21] **I write to you, not because you do not know the truth, but because you know it, and you know that no lie comes from the truth.** [22] **Who is the liar but the one who denies that Jesus is the Christ? This is the antichrist, the one who denies the Father and the Son.** [23] **No one who denies the Son has the Father; everyone who confesses the Son has the Father also.** [24] **Let what you heard from the beginning abide in you. If what you heard from the beginning abides in you, then you will abide in the Son and in the Father.** [25] **And this is what he has promised us, eternal life.**

[26] **I write these things to you concerning those who would deceive you.** [27] **As for you, the anointing that you received from him abides in you, and so you do not need anyone to teach you. But as his anointing teaches you about all things, and is true and is not a lie, and just as it has taught you, abide in him.**

The author once again addresses the readers as his "children," and so begins a new unit (likewise 2:28). As in earlier passages in chapter 2, he speaks directly to the readers at several points (2:20, 24, 27). As before, he speaks in encouraging terms of his reasons for writing: he writes, not because the readers are ignorant, but precisely because they do know the truth (verse 21); he writes about people who deny the Father and the Son, not with reference to the readers, but with reference to "those who would deceive you" (v. 26). This mention of "deceivers and antichrists" (see

2 John 7), however, marks a significant break, the introduction of a new topic and a new set of characters.

Before this point, the author has occasionally hinted at people who do not pass the tests of truth (1:6, 8, 10; 2:4, 9). Now he speaks openly of a particular group of people. There can be no mistaking this for a general reference to just any potential transgressors. This is an actual group that can be pointed out as those who "went out from us," people well known to the readers themselves. Unfortunately, they are not so well known to us, and it requires some work to understand who they were. All the information we have about them is what we can gather from these letters, and I have summarized it in the Introduction to 1 John. In this passage, we learn that they have left the community; that in some way they "deny that Jesus is the Christ"; and perhaps also that they were or sought to be teachers (v. 27). The author also makes several characterizations of them that represent his own evaluation: as teachers, they are really deceivers; in denying Jesus, they are liars who (implicitly) do not have what was heard from the beginning abiding in them; because they left the community, they must not really have belonged to it in the first place.

Above all, the author characterizes these opponents as "antichrists." This term has become so much a part of the Christian vocabulary that it may be surprising to learn that 1 and 2 John are the only writings in the New Testament that use it. Later Christian writers have borrowed it from these letters. Yet our author did not invent the term, since he can assume that the readers have already heard that "antichrist is coming." The Greek word "antichrist" in itself suggests something like "substitute messiah." Other New Testament texts speak of a deceitful opponent or opponents who will arise at the end of time, sometimes calling them false prophets or false messiahs (Matt. 24:4–5, 11, 23–24; 2 Thess. 2:3–12; 2 Peter 2:1; Rev. 13:11–15; 16:13; 19:20; 20:10). The natural tendency is to combine all these figures into one, and the term "antichrist" has come to be applied to this ultimate figure of evil and deception. But we don't really know how such ideas developed in the early church, and there may have been several independent concepts that were later combined into one, rather than one concept expressed in many ways. In particular, there is a difference between a false prophet and a false messiah. The former would be associated with signs and messages supposedly from God; the latter would claim to be a liberator or savior. It is the characteristics of the false prophet that seem more applicable to our author's opponents. They bring a message that they claim is from the Spirit of God but which the author considers a deception; indeed he calls them "false prophets" in 4:1–3. Here, however, perhaps because the subject of their teaching concerned the nature of Christ, he prefers to use the term "antichrist," derived from some otherwise unknown tradition, where it may have meant "false christ" or "substitute messiah."

The author of 1 John transforms the use of the term "antichrist" in three important ways. First, he makes it plural: "many antichrists have come" (since the opponents were not one person but many). Second, he claims that these antichrists have already come, rather than looking for them in the future. Third, he identifies them, not with an arch-deceiver from outside the Christian community, but with rival teachers *within* the community. This is a rather bold set of moves, and the author may conceivably have been in some doubt about whether the readers would accept them. Perhaps partly in order to convince them to do so, and partly because he believes that they will, he writes as if they were definitely on his side in the dispute, contrasting the opponents with "us" (the author and the readers) and with "you" (the readers).

By identifying "the antichrist" with his opponents, the author set a fateful course for the Christian treatment of theological disputes. Again and again, one party in a disagreement has stuck the label "antichrist" onto the other, making their opponents not merely erring human beings but demons and agents of the devil—just as our author demonizes his opponents in chapter 3. The same is true of the author's assertion that "they did not belong to us." One way of dealing with fundamental theological differences is to declare that the members of the other party are simply not true Christians, and never were. Of course, the stakes were high in this dispute, as they often are in theological controversies, and it is hard not to see questions about ultimate issues as entailing ultimate consequences. Yet once such assertions have begun to be made, it becomes easier and easier to do so in smaller and smaller matters, until the devil seems to be lurking behind every minor disagreement.

The claim that the antichrists have already come also brings with it serious consequences, as seen in the opening words of the passage: "Children, it is the last hour!" In the tradition to which the author appeals, the appearance of the antichrist was a sign that the end of time had come (similarly to the other New Testament texts noted above). If his opponents are the fulfillment of that expectation, then the end must have arrived. Such a reading of signs, with or without reference to the antichrist, has happened repeatedly in Christian history since the writing of 1 John. The results have often ranged from the unfortunate to the disastrous. (The latest example of this, of course, was the alarm over the coming of the year

2000.) First John, however, does not urge any specific actions or preparations on the community in view of this arrival, other than avoiding the false teachers. He does not tell the readers to abandon their ordinary lives or to warn their neighbors that they are about to disappear in a "rapture." This is consistent with the fact that, although the early decades of the church were pervaded by a sense of living in the "end times," the impact on most believers was primarily ethical, as their teachers urged them to live lives of great integrity and mutual love in view of the coming end (see, for example, Rom. 13:11–14; 1 Thess. 5:1–11; 1 Peter 4:7–8; note especially 1 Tim. 4:1–2; 2 Tim. 3:1–9). We have seen something of this already in 1 John: the commandment of love is a "new commandment" because it belongs to the dawning light of the new era (2:8); this world is already fading away, and so should have no claim on believers (2:17). The fact that the Messiah had come and that his followers had received the Holy Spirit meant that the early Christians inevitably felt themselves to be living in the final days, when the promises of God were reaching their ultimate fulfillment. Our author, like other early leaders, encourages them to live the life of that messianic age in love for one another, but also to view the rise of dissension and (in his view) questionable teaching in the community as further indications that the end was upon them.

Many Christians today look at the social, cultural, technological, and ecological strains of our time and also conclude that the end must be near. For many others, however, such beliefs have little or no relevance or value any more. It is certainly sobering to see a teacher capable of insights so profound as those found elsewhere in 1 John declaring, after perhaps only 70 years or so of the church's existence, that "it is the last hour." Shall we simply say, "Well, apparently he, and many others, were mistaken," and leave it at that? Shall we suppose that they miscalculated by a millennium or two (or three)? Shall we assume that, whether they knew it or not, they were really writing about our time? Shall we declare that all such assertions inevitably go wrong, and lead the church down a mistaken path? Shall we say that since the Messiah had come, it really was the last hour, only not in the sense that 1 John means? Or shall we try to find something else that the text could possibly mean, so that it would not be in error? These are choices for individual readers to make, and each reader's sense of the possibilities for God's actions, for scripture's fallibility, and for the meanings of texts will condition how she or he interprets. Perhaps the most important thing is to consider what the author advised his original readers to do in light of his conviction that the end was at hand. We will turn to this next, as we consider the rest of this passage.

The author is concerned here about one particular aspect of these "antichrists" whose appearance signaled to him the coming of the last hour, namely, their teaching about Jesus Christ. As in 1:5–2:11, it is a matter of truth and lying. The readers know the truth; the liar denies that Jesus is the Christ. Could some members of this Christian community actually have been denying that Jesus was the Messiah? Of course, that had been precisely the issue between Christians (mainly of Jewish origin) and the many Jews who did not join them in the early days of this community's history. We see this controversy depicted on the screen of Jesus' own life in the Gospel of John, in terms that are sometimes violent (for instance, John 8:39–59; 10:22–39). Given this traumatic prior history, it seems unlikely that many people who belonged to the community would have gone backward into that kind of denial. Rather, in 2 John 9 the opponents are accused of going *forward*. Here, too, the author urges the readers to "let what you heard from the beginning abide in you." Therefore it seems likely that the denial in question refers to something else, some new development that separated the identity of Jesus from that of "the Christ." There were Christian groups with gnostic tendencies in the second century that did something similar to this, and it may be that, like them, 1 John's opponents distinguished between Jesus, the human being, and the Christ, the Son of God, the divine being who came down from heaven. In so doing, they would apparently have seen spiritual significance only in the heavenly Christ, not the human Jesus of flesh and blood.

Further evidence of such tendencies will appear in chapters 4 and 5. At this point, it is enough to know that the opponents offered a teaching about Christ that was, in the author's view, a deviation from "what you heard from the beginning," to such an extent that he considered them to be denying the Son of God—and thereby denying God. For him, to deny that the human Jesus is the Christ, the Son of God, is to deny God, since it is Jesus who made God known (1 John 4:9; 5:20). In order to "have the Father," to know and acknowledge God truly, one must truly know and confess Jesus (1 John 5:12; 2 John 9). How the opponents themselves presented their teaching, of course, we do not know. It may be that our author is describing their beliefs here in his own words. By writing as he does in verses 22–24, he frames the controversy in terms of the confession of faith that had been so central to this community "from the beginning" (note John 20:31). Thus he suggests that the opponents are on the wrong side of the community's history, and so continues to draw the readers toward his perspective.

In this situation, with the community's oneness shattered by the departure of a group, perhaps a fairly large group, who have come to hold a new understanding of Christ—a situation so dire as to be portrayed as "the last hour"—1 John urges those who are left to take a stance of "abiding." They should let the original teaching about Jesus Christ abide in them, and this will allow them to abide in Jesus and in God. This emphasis on abiding suggests a desire for stability and continuity, for maintaining a tradition in the face of serious innovations. Having the traditional teaching abiding in one is probably the same as having God's word or the truth in oneself (1:8, 10; 2:4, 14). The author's ultimate concern, however, is for abiding in Christ and in God, that is, for maintaining a relationship of communion with the divine. Previously, 1 John has spoken of abiding in the divine in terms of walking as Jesus walked and loving one's brother and sister (2:6, 10). Now we are told that a true understanding of Jesus is also necessary for maintaining this relationship. Indeed, "what you heard from the beginning," which in this connection seems to refer to teaching about Jesus, refers to the love commandment in 2:7–11; 3:11. The traditional teaching thus has these two aspects, both of which were apparently violated by the opponents. By abiding both in love and in belief, Christians abide in God (1 John 3:23–24; 4:15–16). The outcome of this relationship of abiding is the promise of God, eternal life.

The readers are urged to let what they have heard abide in them, which is something they can and must do in order to abide in Christ and in God. But they also have an anointing that abides in them and teaches them everything they need to know, teaches them to "abide in him"; and this anointing is not their own doing. It is something that they have "received from him," from "the Holy One" (2:20, 27). Ambiguous references abound here, but the one in whom they abide is surely Jesus (meaning Jesus as they had heard of him from the beginning), who may also be the giver of the anointing (for Jesus as "the Holy One," compare John 6:69; Mark 1:24; Acts 3:14; Rev. 3:7). Elsewhere, however, 1 John refers to God as the giver of the Holy Spirit (3:24; 4:13), and it is the Spirit to which the term "anointing" most likely refers. This word is used in a similar way in 2 Corinthians 1:21–22, and in Luke 4:18 and Acts 10:38, where Jesus is said to have been anointed by God with the Holy Spirit (referring to Isa. 61:1; see also 1 Sam. 16:13). In the Gospel of John, the Spirit is associated with abiding, with "teaching about all things," and with truth (John 14:17, 26; 15:26; 16:13; note also John 4:23–24; 1 John 4:6; 5:6), as is the anointing in verse 27 here. It is the anointing of the Spirit, then, that brings the readers knowledge, that teaches and has taught them to abide in Jesus. This anointing is not something that the readers generate within themselves, but is a gift of God.

This divine gift continues to teach the believers the truth, and only the truth. Since lying is identified with the opponents' teaching about Christ, this truth that the readers have been taught by the Spirit must mean the teaching "from the beginning" that the human Jesus is the divine Son of God (2:20–22). Their faithfulness to this teaching, then, is not only a matter of persistence on their own part, but of the Spirit's activity within and among them. The Spirit is their teacher, and they need no other. Here again we may see the life of the church understood as the fulfillment of God's promises (Isa. 54:13; Jer. 31:33–34). With God's Spirit to teach them directly, the community does not need instruction in the nature of Christ, and certainly not from the opponents; for what the Spirit teaches will remain faithful to the truth heard from the beginning, that Jesus is the Christ, the Son of God. But the author is walking a tightrope here, for if the community does not need *any* human teacher, then it does not need him either! Yet he clearly does write in the manner of a teacher, addressing the readers as his "children" (compare Prov. 5:1; 7:24; 8:32). If they take seriously their competence, as anointed by the Spirit, to know and understand all that is needed, then they may well feel that they need not listen to the elder's urgings any more than to those of his opponents.

There are tensions in this passage that have continued to be at work in the history of the Christian church through all its ages. One of these tensions is between authoritative teachers and the freedom of the individual believer to be taught by God. Another is between the force of tradition, "what you heard from the beginning," and innovative responses to new circumstances. The author says, "Listen to the tradition, and listen to the Spirit." But what if voices claiming the Spirit seek to modify the tradition? There can be little doubt that the opponents also claimed to have the Spirit behind their innovations (note 1 John 4:1–6); and they were not completely without justification in doing so. They may have appealed to a tradition such as the one found in John 14:25–26 and 16:12–13, which promises precisely that the Spirit will guide the community into truth not given them earlier. Throughout Christian history, the Spirit has often been claimed as a force challenging traditional teachings and institutions, while the church's teaching authorities have often invoked tradition in order to limit both appeals to the Spirit and the interpretive freedom of individual believers. What we see in these letters are some of the earliest recorded instances of such conflicts. First John asserts that claims to be guided by the Spirit must be evaluated according to traditional teaching; yet he does not establish any teaching authority to override individual assertions of instruction by the Spirit.

The various Christian denominations have sorted out this problem in different ways. Authority may be located in a church hierarchy, in a gathering of church officials, in the assembled representatives of the body of believers, or in the pastors of local congregations. It may be located in traditional statements of faith, or solely in the Bible, or in the individual believer who reads the Bible. It is often located in some combination of these things. In every case, though, the guidance of the Spirit of God is claimed for the authoritative text, tradition, or persons. New movements often begin with individuals claiming authority from the Spirit to overturn the traditional authorities or claiming to represent a recovery of the tradition's original intent. Churches that today seem highly conservative often began as radical breaks with conservative belief and practice. First John places us right in the midst of these very troubled waters.

The assertion that the Spirit is the only teacher that Christians need suggests a vision of the church that is close to anarchy; at any rate, it is far removed from the hierarchical end of the spectrum, and far toward the egalitarian end. Yet 1 John also asserts that believers must remain faithful to the traditional teaching heard from the beginning. Tradition and Spirit are thus brought into a relationship, not of tension, but of mutual support. The author is convinced that the Spirit will not lead in a direction fundamentally different from that of the tradition, and that the tradition will not stifle the voice of the Spirit. Both Spirit and tradition lead toward the goal of maintaining communion with the divine, abiding in God and in Jesus. The tradition determines what can rightly be claimed as coming from the Spirit; yet the tradition itself is not maintained by institutional authorities, but by the work of the Spirit in individual believers. We may wonder whether such an understanding could remain stable for very long. Yet it represents a vision of Christian freedom that remains both loyal to the past and open to the Spirit's leading, and a vision of Christian tradition that allows for elasticity without losing the shape of the tradition altogether.

The author's appeal to "what you heard from the beginning" may be seen as paving the way for two later directions in the Christian understanding of authority: a canon of scripture embodying the earliest teachings of the church, and church tradition as the final judge of truth. But we must note that this appeal speaks neither of authoritative writings nor of "tradition" as such. First John's ultimate appeal is to the truth itself. The author does not defend the tradition simply because it is traditional, but because he believes it embodies the truth about Jesus Christ, both human and divine, the truth that enables one to abide in God and to have eternal life. It is this truth, the truth of the incarnation, that is the real authority for the author of 1 John.

THE CHILDREN OF GOD
1 John 2:28–3:10

2:28 **And now, little children, abide in him, so that when he is revealed we may have confidence and not be put to shame before him at his coming.** 29 **If you know that he is righteous, you may be sure that everyone who does right has been born of him.** 3:1 **See what love the Father has given us, that we should be called children of God; and that is what we are. The reason the world does not know us is that it did not know him.** 2 **Beloved, we are God's children now; what we will be has not yet been revealed. What we do know is this: when he is revealed, we will be like him, for we will see him as he is.** 3 **And all who have this hope in him purify themselves, just as he is pure.**

4 **Everyone who commits sin is guilty of lawlessness; sin is lawlessness.** 5 **You know that he was revealed to take away sins, and in him there is no sin.** 6 **No one who abides in him sins; no one who sins has either seen him or known him.** 7 **Little children, let no one deceive you. Everyone who does what is right is righteous, just as he is righteous.** 8 **Everyone who commits sin is a child of the devil; for the devil has been sinning from the beginning. The Son of God was revealed for this purpose, to destroy the works of the devil.** 9 **Those who have been born of God do not sin, because God's seed abides in them; they cannot sin, because they have been born of God.** 10 **The children of God and the children of the devil are revealed in this way: all who do not do what is right are not from God, nor are those who do not love their brothers and sisters.**

This passage, right in the middle of 1 John, in many ways typifies the problems it can present. At first glance, its statements are simple, if not simplistic. It would be easy to read through it and nod in affirmation at every verse. But then we reach 3:8 and perhaps begin to feel a little uneasy. Verses 9 and 10 are likely to increase this uneasiness still further. If we go back and look carefully at the entire passage, we begin to find vagueness in the grammar, difficult complexities in the structure, and nearly insoluble puzzles in the thinking. Yet those comforting and encouraging simplicities remain, almost seeming to gaze back at us and ask, "What is the problem, after all?"

To begin with the grammatical difficulties, we find our author once again speaking of "abiding in him," "when he is revealed," "being born of him," and so on, without ever specifying who is meant by "him." As in other passages, we may have here in part a series of familiar formulas, not too carefully connected. The one of whom we are born must be God, since the passage speaks explicitly of "children of God." The one who is to be revealed and who was revealed is surely Jesus. Indeed, the Greek pronoun translated "he" in 3:3, 5, 7 is used in 1 John to refer only to Jesus, and always in reference to imitating him, a grammatical oddity in itself. The most serious identity ambiguities are in 2:29 and 3:2. Verse 28 clearly speaks of Jesus, but by the end of verse 29 the reference has shifted to God. The question is, To whom does "he is righteous" refer? The answer may well be Jesus, though it may not make much difference to the meaning. The difficulty and its significance for interpretation are greater in the second half of 3:2. Here, "when he is revealed" could just as well, and perhaps better, be translated "when *it* is revealed," that is, when "what we will be" is revealed, continuing from the first half of the verse. In that case, the one whom we will see and be like is most probably God.

The whole passage is filled with such a variety of structural devices that it is hard to know just what structure the author intended. For instance, running through the passage is a series of statements that begin with "everyone who," "all who," "no one who," "those who. . . ." All these statements have the same grammatical form in the Greek, and most of them can be lined up in contrasting pairs (3:6 is the most obvious example). Another approach to the structure of the passage is more thematic. A new paragraph may begin at verse 7, where the author starts over with "Little children" (rather than at verse 4 with the NRSV). In the first paragraph (2:28–3:6), the author speaks first of those who "do right" (2:28–3:3) and then of those who "commit sin" (3:4–6). The same expressions appear in the second paragraph (3:7–10), but in a more elaborate sequence. First we read of those who "do what is right," then of those who "commit sin." Following a statement on the purpose of Christ's coming, we read next of those who "do *not* sin," and finally of those who "do *not* do what is right." This way of understanding the structure of the passage brings out its major theme: the contrast between two groups of people and two ways of acting.

This major theme is treated through the use of several other themes that run through the passage. These themes are: the children of God; righteousness and sin; being like Jesus and God; and revelation. We can get an overall picture of what the author is saying by focusing on these themes; but we will also need to give special consideration to the particular difficulties of the question of sinlessness in this passage and elsewhere in 1 John.

One of the two groups of people contrasted in this passage is the group called "*the children of God*" (3:1, 2, 10). The author intends to give the readers clear-cut tests for recognizing those who are and are not God's children. In chapter 5, he will specify correct belief in Jesus as one of these tests, as in the Gospel of John (John 1:12–13). Here, though, the test is right actions. But neither the Gospel nor the letters of John make any effort to spell out the "mechanics" of how people become children of God.

We may presume that it is because God gives life to those who believe in Jesus (John 3:16; 11:25–26; 20:31; 1 John 5:11) that believers are called God's "children"; but we do not learn anything about an exact sequence of events that must take place, or how the divine will and the human will interact in this process (John 6:36–47). Instead, these texts are much more concerned with the *results* of being "born of God." We may note one thing, however, that our author does say about the cause of believers' becoming children of God: it is due to God's love. It was not anything they did or anything unusual about them; it was God's doing, purely as an act of love.

For 1 John, the main result of being God's child has to do with righteousness, as will be seen shortly. There is another result, however, and that has to do with "the world." As we saw in discussing 2:15–17, "the world," as 1 John uses it in 3:1, means, not the natural creation, but the system of human society that maintains an organized opposition to its Creator, centering on itself and its own gratification rather than on God's will of mutual love. Since the world fails to know God, it fails to know those who come from God—both Jesus (John 7:28–29; 8:19, 54–55) and those who are God's children because of Jesus (John 15:18–16:3; 17:14–16). (It is typical of 1 John, however, that it does not speak of Jesus but simply of God as the cause of the world's ignorance of believers.) This understanding of the believing community in relation to "the outside world" is common in countercultural groups and the communities that sociologists define as "sects," groups that are relatively closed off, often due to rejection of their message and persecution by the dominant society. Mainstream Christianity today seldom has this sense about itself. However, some smaller denominations do, and even some relatively well-situated groups and leaders foster a sense of cultural isolation, sometimes even while claiming to represent a societal majority and seeking to gain political power. First John is not interested in taking over the world. Instead, it reflects the circumstances of the early church, often finding itself severely harassed because of its lack of conformity to traditional social values. Problematic as this attitude toward the world may seem today, it was part of what enabled those churches to survive.

Besides children of God, the text also speaks of "children of the devil" in 3:10. Verse 8 in the Greek simply says, "The one who commits sin is of the devil," with the NRSV adding "a child"; but even here, there is probably a reference to John 8:44, which contains a similar idea. Yet 1 John has even less to say about how people become children of the devil than it does about the children of God. The author seems uninterested in the possible origins of the reality he observes, whether in cosmic history or in divine predestination. He simply wants to point out the existence of the two sets of "offspring," and emphasize the tests by which they may be recognized. This leaves us in no position to speculate about how he *might* have conceived the process by which people become children of God or of the devil, much as we might wish to know that. Instead, we must simply direct our attention to those tests that set the two groups apart.

The test highlighted here is that of conduct, expressed in terms of *righteousness and sin*, terms that are so pervasive in this passage that they helped us above in determining its structure. The author does little to define these concepts in the abstract (the end of 3:4 may be concerned to identify sin with the lawlessness expected to appear in the last days; compare Matt. 24:12; 2 Thess. 2:3–12). Instead, he speaks of *doing* righteousness and sin (rendered "doing [what is] right" and "committing sin" ["sinning" in 3:9] by the NRSV). It is the action, not the abstract quality, that interests 1 John. Nevertheless, these remain very broad terms, which may lead us to think in general terms of good and bad conduct. It should be remembered, however, that "righteousness" represents a Greek word that can often be translated "justice," suggesting that the author is not thinking in terms of a purely personal morality.

In fact, he virtually provides a definition of "righteousness" in 3:10, which brings the picture into full clarity. "Doing what is right" is equivalent to "loving one's brothers and sisters." (Since being able to "do righteousness" is a characteristic of the children of God, we should note that 1 John 4:7 also associates being born of God with love.) Those who are God's children do what is right, that is, they love one another. For 1 John, at least, righteousness does not consist of moral goodness in general or of following a list of ethical instructions or of maintaining the traditional values of society (which this author might be more inclined to identify with "the world"). It means love—just as the only commandment specifically noted in 2:3–11 is the new commandment of love, and just as the God who is "faithful and just [in other words, righteous]" (1:9) is also identified as love (4:7–18). The author is no more interested in defining love than in other abstract discussions; but the basic nature of the love that he urges on his readers can be seen in 3:16–17. It leads to the giving up of one's own interests for the sake of others, even to the point of laying down one's life.

That understanding of love is based on the actions of Jesus, and the theme of *being like or imitating Jesus and God* is as prominent in this passage as anywhere in 1 John. The readers know that the righteous are born of God because Jesus (or perhaps God) is righteous. The world does not know these children of God because it did not know God. When our final nature is revealed, it will be like that of God (or perhaps Jesus); but even now we should make ourselves pure like Jesus. Since there is no sin in Jesus, those who abide in him do not sin. They do what is right, and are righteous, as he is. Of course, the righteousness of Christians is not based on their own efforts, but on their being children of God. They do not "do what is right" in order to become God's children; they do it *because they are* God's children. Yet, paradoxically, doing right does involve personal choice and action. Children of God have been given God's love (3:1), but only in order to give that love to one another. In this "doing what is right," believers model their actions on the actions of others—not those of successful people or of happy people or even of other Christians, but the actions of Jesus, and indeed of God. Perhaps they need not be without a place to lay their heads, like the Son of Man (Luke 9:57–58); but they are expected to take up the cross like him (Mark 8:34–35). Certainly they are not expected to know like God or to exercise power like God; but they are called to love like God (1 John 4:7–18).

No one in their right mind would deny the enormous moral challenge here. Yet it is a challenge with which God's people have always been faced. The section of the book of Leviticus known as the "Holiness Code" urges the Israelites to be holy as God is holy (Lev. 11:44–45; 19:2; 20:26; 21:8). Jesus supported this call to the imitation of God, but he transformed its content. He taught people that, rather than imitating God's holiness, they ought to be *merciful* as God is merciful (Luke 6:35–36; Matt. 18:23–34). The Gospel and letters of John continue Jesus' teaching in their own way, by focusing on self-giving love as the way to be like him (besides the passages in 1 John, see John 12:24–26; 13:34–35; 15:12–13). For this reason, we may assume that when the author encourages the readers to "purify themselves, just as he is pure," he is not reverting to the thought-world of Leviticus, but is still speaking of love, the one attribute of Jesus on which he focuses. The New Testament letters, like other ancient religious writings, often use purity as a metaphor for moral action (Phil. 4:8; 1 Tim. 4:12; 1 Peter 1:22; 3:2). In the literal sense, ritual purity was necessary to enter the presence of God (Exod. 19:10–11; Ps. 24:3–4), and the metaphor could also be used in this way (Matt. 5:8; James 4:8). Thus all who hope to see God in reality must "purify" themselves (1 John 3:2–3). Our author adds a unique note, however, in speaking of Jesus as "pure," for this term is not applied to Jesus or to God anywhere else in the Bible. Evidently he does so in order to maintain the theme of Jesus as our model for imitation.

The children of God are to be like the Son of God: this is the simple, yet so profoundly difficult, wellspring of the ethical message of 1 John. In one sense, this likeness is a matter of "family resemblance"; the ability to love is given with one's birth from God, just as I inherited some skill at writing from my mother. Yet it is also a matter of *imitation*, of seeking to be like the One whose children we are, and like Jesus our brother. Recently, the slogan "What Would Jesus Do?" has swept through many Christian circles (though it is the nature of such fads that by the time you read this it may already have evaporated). One can even see "WWJD" on bumper stickers and jewelry. Whatever its real value, this craze does at least represent an authentic motif in Christian spirituality and ethics, one well attested in 1 John. The New Testament does call on us to ask ourselves what Jesus would do, and to act accordingly. The one constant with which it presents us is that whatever we might imagine Jesus doing must be tested against the standard of self-giving love that he both taught and practiced. This extends from large-scale decisions about where we live and what we do for a living, through what we eat, wear, and drive, all the way down to whether we hit the brake or the gas when the light turns yellow. We should never suppose that "What would Jesus do?" is a question that replaces all other questions. Rather, it opens up a whole host of questions, and it will not leave us alone until it penetrates every aspect of our lives, both the most private and the most public. It is the least superficial question in the world, and if we ask it superficially, we run the risk of getting an answer beyond our wildest imagination.

The fourth theme running through this passage is that of *revelation*. Interestingly, this revelation is spoken of in terms of past, present, and future. The Son of God was revealed to take away sins, destroying the work of the devil (3:5, 8). In the present, the children of God and of the devil are revealed by their actions, showing their resemblance to their "parents" (3:10). And, ultimately, Jesus will be revealed again at his second coming; then the true destiny of God's children will be revealed as well (2:28; 3:2). Revelation is thus linked to the other three themes and appears in all the structural divisions of this passage. At his first revelation, Christ made it possible for children of God to be free from sin, and at his second they will be revealed in their likeness to God. In the meantime, their identity is revealed already in their likeness to Jesus, in whom there is no sin. The theme of revelation is used to emphasize the continuity between the first coming of Christ and his second coming, and between what the children of God are in the present and will be at the end.

Of course, prior to this 1 John has stressed that the end is already dawning, the world is passing away, the last hour has come (2:8, 17, 18). Here we see this sense of living at the turning point of the ages modified some-what by an attitude that looks forward to an end that is yet to come. In this 1 John more closely resembles many other New Testament writings (except the Gospel of John), even using some of the terminology that is common elsewhere, namely, the language of Jesus' being "revealed" at the end (Col. 3:4; 1 Peter 5:4) and of his "coming" (for example, Matt. 24:3, 27, 37, 39; 1 Thess. 3:13; 5:23). It also resembles Paul in particular in speaking of the transformation of Christians to a higher state at the return of Christ (1 Cor. 13:12; 15:51–53; Phil. 3:20–21). It may be that our author's opponents claimed to have a direct vision of God or of Christ already, or claimed that the Spirit had already made them completely like Christ. If so, part of his point here is that that vision and transformation cannot really be reached now. Indeed, the opponents' resemblance to Christ lacks the most essential feature, his love for others, which would suggest that their vision of him is false. It would also suggest that, so far from being what the children of God will ultimately be, they are not even what God's children can be now.

For this author also, however, there is an element of truth in saying that Christians already live the life of the end times. The Messiah has come, and those who believe in him become children of God, as he is the Son of God, and love as he loved, putting into practice the mutual love that char-acterizes the new, messianic era. The resemblance to him that they thus display is a foretaste of the resemblance to God that they will ultimately enjoy. The love they exercise now is the result of the love God has given them, and a harbinger of the love to come.

This passage, interweaving a number of themes in a complex set of pat-terns, sets out criteria for distinguishing between children of God and children of the devil; or rather, it sets out one single criterion. Look for the family resemblance, it says; and that resemblance can be seen in how people live their lives, how they act. The likeness is neither a hidden one that will not be revealed at all until the last day, nor an identity that is already so close that no further transformation could be needed. It is also not a matter of superficial customs and conventions, a dress code or a lifestyle. The children of God are revealed now as they will be at the end, by their likeness to God and to God's Son Jesus Christ, which means by their righteousness—that is, by their love.

One very serious question remains before we leave this passage. How can the writer say, "Those who have been born of God do not sin," indeed, "they *cannot* sin"? The statement seems implausible enough all by itself. Coming from an author who has already said, "If we say that we have no sin, we deceive ourselves," and "If we say that we have not sinned, we make [God] a liar" (1:8, 10), it creates an intolerable contradiction. What is the answer? Can Christians sin or can't they?

Not surprisingly, an enormous variety of solutions to this problem has been proposed. Perhaps the conflicting passages are talking about two different kinds of sin; or represent two different types of perfectionism; or they alternate between idealism and practicality. Perhaps the author only means to speak here of a *possibility* of not sinning that must then be put into practice; or of a process of transformation; or of a community that might be sinless rather than sinless individuals; or of a concept similar to Martin Luther's doctrine that Christians are both righteous and sinful at the same time. Perhaps grammatical differences between the passages mean the author is trying to say that Christians do not *habitually* sin, though they may commit single *acts* of sin. Unfortunately, there is really no evidence in any of the passages in question that any of these is what the author intends. There is no consistent grammatical distinction between the "can sin" and "can't sin" passages. Even if some distinction could be drawn between two different areas of thought in the contradictory texts, the texts still contradict each other. The author flatly says at one point that Christians should confess their sins, for which Jesus makes atonement, and at another point that they do not sin at all. In fact, in 1 John 5:16–18 he says both things side by side!

Assuming that the author intended to make sense, he may have meant to say simply that Christian life is a paradox, that we know we are set free from sin, and yet we find ourselves caught up in it still. Perhaps, when we find contradictions in our own lives, we ought to take some comfort in the presence of equally perplexing contradictions in the sacred scriptures. In this sense, the text reflects the condition of human life, never able to reach perfection, and yet never able to keep from trying. Perhaps in that very spirit, then, we ought to try a bit more to understand these contradictory passages.

Because the position advocated in 3:9—that Christians do not and cannot sin—is so very much like the one rejected in 1:8–10, it is possible that it actually originated with the author's opponents and that he is taking up that position only to refine it and seek some other sense in which it might be true. The opponents may have claimed that through Christ, the Spirit had transformed them and made them either incapable of sinning or at least not subject to any guilt for sinning. They could have based this on the very ideas that the author puts forward in 3:5: Christ came to take away sins (specific acts of sin), and there is no sin (as a general principle) in him.

If so, then the author's debate with them concerned the meaning of these ideas. The opponents would have been saying that as Christians, they were in principle sinless. Mere external actions would not affect this sinlessness in principle. Our author responds that actions are what really counts, and that Christian sinlessness is not a matter of principle but of practice. People who have truly been transformed demonstrate that transformation in their freedom from concrete acts of sin. The opponents asked, "Who is sinless?," and answered, "The children of God," meaning those who resemble God in their inner spiritual perfection. The author asks, "Who are the children of God?," and answers "Those who do not sin," meaning those who resemble God in their acts of love for one another. The opponents may have been saying that connection with God determines everything else, perhaps using an expression like "children of God" in a fairly literal sense. The author uses the same language to say that it is conduct that demonstrates connection with God. (Note that he does not say that the children of the devil *must* inevitably sin.) Of course, in the author's view this question and this answer would exclude the opponents themselves, and that is no doubt part of what he aims to do.

The claim of sinlessness, whether it originates with the author or with his opponents, is based on the fact of birth from God. In this understanding, sinlessness is not an ideal for which Christians should strive, but the result of a divine element planted within them, which the author calls "God's seed." This expression, unheard of elsewhere in the Bible, is similar to terminology used by gnostics, which could be another indicator that 1 John has borrowed it from the opponents. It uses the metaphor of human sperm to depict what we might call the genetic resemblance between Christians and God, and to claim that this resemblance keeps them from sinning. A modern writer might say, "Those who have been born of God do not sin, because God's DNA abides in them." But what does the metaphor really mean? What is the divine element implanted in the children of God? Elsewhere, 1 John speaks of God's word abiding in believers (1:10; 2:14; note also 2:24). But we also read of God's anointing, the Spirit, that abides in them (2:27; note also 3:24; 4:13), and the Spirit seems more likely to be the agent of birth from God in this tradition (John 3:5–8). If this is correct (and it is by no means certain), then it is the Spirit abiding in Christians that keeps them from sinning.

This difficult text, which contradicts not only common experience but what the same author writes elsewhere, may never be fully understood. In some way, it is most likely related to 1 John's controversy with opponents who claimed to be so much God's spiritual children that they were free from sin, and yet did not carry out the acts of love that, in our author's view, are the only adequate demonstration of such a claim. God's children may indeed sin, he says in 1:5–2:2 and 5:16–17; and if they do, they have the faithfulness of God, the blood and the intercession of Christ, and the prayers of their brothers and sisters to redeem them. Yet the Spirit who gave them birth from God abides within them, and makes a genuine spiritual transformation possible, one that will demonstrate who the true children of God are by the acts of love that characterize the day-to-day realities of their lives. We may find it hard to agree, viewing our own lives and those of others around us, that "those who have been born of God do not sin." We ought to find it easier to admit that the new birth of Christian life does bring with it a transformation that is neither purely hypothetical nor so personal that it cannot be seen by other people. The children of God are discovered when people see Christians loving one another in concrete ways. That, at any rate, we may confidently take away from this passage.

LOVE AND HATE
1 John 3:11–17

3:11 **For this is the message you have heard from the beginning, that we should love one another.** [12] **We must not be like Cain who was from the evil one and murdered his brother. And why did he murder him? Because his own deeds were evil and his brother's righteous.** [13] **Do not be astonished, brothers and sisters, that the world hates you.** [14] **We know that we have passed from death to life because we love one another. Whoever does not love abides in death.** [15] **All who hate a brother or sister are murderers, and you know that murderers do not have eternal life abiding in them.** [16] **We know love by this, that he laid down his life for us—and we ought to lay down our lives for one another.** [17] **How does God's love abide in anyone who has the world's goods and sees a brother or sister in need and yet refuses help?**

The theme of love, which first appeared in 2:9–11, was reintroduced in 3:10. Now it is brought to the forefront, and it will remain there through the end of chapter 4. This passage is marked off by the opening reference to "the message you have heard from the beginning," and by the address "Little children" in 3:18, which makes a transition to the next unit. After the introductory 3:11, the themes of love and hate, self-giving and murder alternate, with hate and murder dominating in 3:12–15 and love and self-giving in 3:16–17. In the middle of the passage, these two subsections are held together by the theme of knowing in 3:14–16.

There are a number of continuities between this passage and the preceding one, beginning with the obvious fact that 3:11 provides a reason for the statement in 3:10. In discussing 3:8, I noted that it probably makes a reference to John 8:44; this reference is taken up again in 3:12, 15. The sharp contrasts of the preceding passage are also continued, but are worked out in different terms. The children of God and of the devil are exemplified by Jesus and Cain; righteousness and sin are specified as love and hate (an opposition that also appeared in 2:9–11), self-giving and murder. A new contrast, life and death, is also introduced. As we have seen at several points, 1 John seems to have no room for a middle ground or for shades of gray. Whatever is not love is hatred. Love means giving up one's own life for the sake of someone else; hatred means the taking of someone else's life, that is, murder. This mode of thinking, with its rigid and absolute contrasts, is not a familiar or comfortable one for many people today. Yet, to a culture that has come almost to cherish a sense of ambiguity pervading all of life's circumstances, 1 John provides a healthy reminder that there are choices that can be made, and that some choices bring us closer to God while others do not.

First John has spoken before about the message that the readers have heard long since. In 1:5 that message was about God: God is light. In 3:11 it is about us: we should love one another. The similarity in form between 1:5 and 3:11 seems to suggest that the two messages are equivalent. Moreover, the word translated "message" is similar to one used elsewhere in the New Testament and translated "gospel" or "good news." Though 1 John also speaks of love as a commandment (2:7–11; 3:23; 4:21), here love for one another is presented virtually as the gospel, the fundamental Christian message of good news about the love of God. For this author, then, *love is not law, but gospel.* The good news is not only that God's love for us has been made known in Jesus Christ, but also that God's children love one another. The realm of love is made available to those who believe in Jesus; they become a community of those who love one another. This is the message that the community proclaims, not only to the world but, as here, to itself. This means that the concept of "good works" takes on a different aspect from what we may be used to, based on an exaggerated interpretation of Galatians. Doing is not merely the outcome of faith, it *is* faith; for the love for one another that is the Christian message is a matter not of abstract emotion but of concrete action. The equation runs equally well in both directions: to believe in Jesus is to love one another; to love one another is to believe in Jesus; for it is Jesus Christ who brought divine love fully into the world, and believing in him means accepting love as the way of life given by God.

The opposite of love is hate, and just as in 2:18–27 the author claims that his opponents have denied the gospel message that Jesus is the Christ, here it is probably also the same opponents whom he regards as having turned away from the gospel message of love in favor of hate. They have left the community of love; they may have left off supporting the poor (see the discussion of 3:17 below). That is enough (for this author) to put them on the side of hatred. As one way of making this clear to the readers, he makes a series of references to the tradition that all members of this Christian community held in common, a tradition that is primarily contained in the Gospel of John. In the process, he attempts to make it clear that the opponents (who likely also laid claim to it) have misinterpreted this tradition. The most obvious example of this citation of tradition is the message of love, which the community has had "from the beginning" (John 13:34–35; 15:12, 17). Above, I noted the reference to John 8:44 in the mention of a murderer who is "from the evil one." The claim that "we have passed from death to life" (3:14) is almost a direct quotation of John 5:24. The reference to "evil deeds" (3:12) is reminiscent of John 3:19–21 and 7:7. The latter verse speaks of the world's hatred of Jesus; its corresponding hatred of Christians (here in 3:13) is comparable to John 15:18–20; 17:14. The expression "lay down one's life" is not found anywhere in the New Testament except in 1 John 3:16 and John 10:11–18 and 15:13. The references to what "we know" and what "you know" in 3:14–16 also serve to enhance the appeal to familiar information. By packing so many allusions to the community's tradition into this short passage, the author seeks to make it clear that his teaching is in the strongest continuity with that tradition, while that of his opponents has abandoned the path in which the community has always walked.

In the Gospel of John, it is the world that does evil deeds, hates Jesus and his followers, and seeks to take his life and their lives (John 16:2). Jesus, by contrast, lays down his life out of love, and so provides an example of righteous deeds for his disciples to imitate. If the opponents have abandoned mutual love, then they have put themselves on the wrong side of the community's tradition, on the side of the world and its hatred, rather than that of Jesus and love. The readers, by contrast, are pictured as being the objects of the world's hatred, and so are placed on the side of Jesus and his disciples. The assumption is that they, unlike the opponents, carry out works of love, the righteous deeds of the children of God (1 John

3:7–10); and this places them on the side of the author, where he wishes them to be.

Where does Cain come into all of this? He is presented as a well-known example, the first example, of hatred and murder, just as Jesus is the premier example of love and self-giving. (Such use of examples was common in the persuasive rhetoric of the time.) The author is referring, of course, to Genesis 4:1–8, where Cain kills his brother Abel. But he also makes use of later traditions that were familiar to both Jewish and Christian interpreters. Genesis, for instance, says nothing about Cain's deeds being evil and Abel's being righteous; but Matthew 23:35 and Hebrews 11:4 hint at a widespread tradition, found in many ancient Jewish writings, that this was the case. Similarly, the assertion that "Cain . . . was from the evil one" may mean more than that he was a "child of the devil" in the moral sense of 1 John 3:8, 10. According to some Jewish legendary traditions, the devil seduced Eve and was the real father of Cain. In these traditions, Cain, because of his parentage, became the first heretic as well as the first murderer. Given this background, Cain's murder of Abel would only be what one would expect, since his father also "was a murderer from the beginning" (John 8:44). Such creation and use of legendary traditions was a common feature in ancient biblical exegesis, which was less concerned with exact historical accuracy than with poetic, moral, and theological truth.

Cain thus furnishes the model for those who do not love their brothers and sisters. Because they come from the evil one, they do evil deeds; the sight of the good deeds done by their brothers and sisters only provokes them to hatred and murder. "All who hate a brother or sister are murderers" (3:15). No doubt the author, addressing the readers as "brothers and sisters" in verse 13, expects them to see themselves as the potential objects of such murder—from their very own brothers and sisters, namely, the unloving opponents. All this is part of our author's habit of thinking in terms of absolute contrasts (a habit he shares with other New Testament writers; compare Eph. 2:1–3; 4:17–18; 6:12). His sweeping equation of lack of love with murder may not strike us as a realistic description of anyone, short of the extreme case of an Adolf Hitler. Yet it is not that far from the words of the Sermon on the Mount in Matthew 5:21–22. Violence has remained an obstinate problem in human societies, and examples, not only of "intimate" murders, but of insane mass killings actually seem to be multiplying in our day. My own city has seen two of the latter in the very month in which I write these words. For 1 John, it all boils down to two possibilities, love and hate. Is that the kind of extremism and absolutism that leads to extremes of violence? Or have we let ourselves become too comfortable with ambiguity, where decisiveness is required? Is not the call of Jesus a call to extreme love, to love even of enemies, to the bearing of the cross? In a time when violence abounds, perhaps we are called upon to take an absolute stand, to support and to participate in every act of self-giving love, to condemn and to resist every threat against human life and every act of violence.

The emphatic "we" at the beginning of verse 14 makes a deliberate contrast between the Cain-like world and "us," that is, the author and the readers who are assumed to belong to his side in the conflict. To "pass from death to life," in the Gospel of John, requires acceptance of Jesus' mission from God (John 5:24). For 1 John, this means living in mutual love, since Jesus' mission was precisely to make known God's love, a love that calls us to love one another in response (1 John 4:7–11). It is those who love one another, then, who have "passed from death to life"; those who do not love "abide in death." In the theology of the Gospel and letters of John, this means that eternal life, the life to be given by God to those who are raised from the dead at the Last Judgment, is already available to those who believe in Jesus and join the community of love. As in 1 John 2:8, the blessings of the last days, the messianic era, are already given with the coming of Jesus the Messiah, who himself was raised from the dead. Hence the Fourth Gospel can speak of Jesus as "the Resurrection and the Life" (John 11:25). Those who reject the Messiah Jesus and his way of love, however, miss the opportunity of eternal life: they "abide in death," remaining in the world that rejects its Creator and Redeemer, and is permeated with hatred and murder instead of love. For 1 John, this means that the opponents, who somehow separate the human Jesus from the divine Christ (Messiah) and have left the community, have put themselves on the wrong side of the community's traditional understanding of eternal life.

Those who love have passed from death to life. Yet the nature of love is such that they are not exempt from suffering, or even from death itself. Far from it: it is precisely by laying down their lives for one another that they follow the example of Jesus, who demonstrated what love really is (3:16). His self-giving death shows that love is more than warm feelings or soothing words or an uplifting doctrine. The New Testament in general does not think of love in terms of feelings but of actions (note 1 John 3:18). Jesus' teaching "Love your enemies" does not mean that we should somehow conjure up pleasant thoughts and sweet affections for those who hate us. It means that we should *do* for them what we do for the people we love: pray for them, give to them, do good to them, show mercy to them as God has shown mercy to us (Luke 6:27–36). No one can generate kind feelings by willpower or on demand; but anyone can perform the actions of love, if they are willing. It is the will to *act* in love, to do good, that is required, not a particular emotion.

Does the writer of 1 John really expect that his readers will need to lay down their lives for one another? That is certainly not out of the question; but there is no indication in these letters that the community is suffering persecution and literally in danger of death. Verse 17 does offer one specific example of the kind of self-giving action that the author is looking for. Perhaps it was the most needed action in the community's current circumstances: caring for the poor among them. Here the question of feelings does come up. The rather bland "refuses help" in the NRSV stands for a clause that could be translated somewhat more literally, "shuts his heart against them." The implication is that refusal to help begins with refusal of compassion, a closing down of the inner self, a turning away of the heart from those in need. But it is not only the heart that is closed off; it is also one's possessions. The word translated "goods" is also rendered "riches" in 2:16. There, it was not the things themselves but the attitude of pride and desire concerning them that was the problem. Here it is not only an attitude but the resulting actions that cut one off from God's love. To have and not to give—for 1 John, this is a fundamental contradiction of the love that leads from death to life. One strong component of the ancient Jewish hope for the world's transformation by God at the end of time was justice for those who had been oppressed and deprived under the status quo. The community of Jesus, the Messiah, the bringer of the new era of eternal life, could not overlook the needs of those within it who were poor. Their poverty may have been due to the world's still unredeemed condition, but the believers were no longer of that world. Now they were of God, and God is love, and love is action for those in need of help. If the opponents refused this help—perhaps because they felt that the life they had received from the spiritual Christ was a spiritual matter, unrelated to material things—they only showed how far they were from the true Christ, the human Jesus who gave up all for us.

There are certainly places on earth today where Christians are genuinely at risk of having to lay down their lives for one another. This commentary is not being written in one of them, and it is a dangerous deception for materially and socially comfortable Christians to fantasize persecutions for themselves. A United States Secretary of the Interior some years ago, having made some bigoted remark in public, tried to make up for it by saying that he understood how oppressed groups feel, since he himself was "a persecuted evangelical Christian." A man who can ride to work in a limousine every morning is not persecuted, and neither are most Christians in the "developed world," however much they may sometimes feel at odds with their society. But even if literal martyrdom is not on the agenda for us, we can actively seek out ways to give our lives for others.

There is no shortage of examples before us. It may be a health care worker who chooses to work long hours among the poor and chronically ill. It may be a teacher who stays in the inner city or the isolated country rather than seeking a university career. It may be an activist who gives up a middle-class career to run a shelter for the homeless, a haven for abused women, or a recovery program for addicts. The center of Christian ethics, beginning with the teaching of Jesus, has always been the surrender of our own interests for the sake of others. The way to life passes through death, not only Jesus' death but our own death (Matt. 10:38–39; Mark 8:34–37; 10:29–31; Luke 14:26–27; 17:33; John 12:24–26; 15:12–13). The death we must die is to our self-interest, our self-concern, that which places our needs and desires at the center of the universe, or at any rate at the center of our lives. That center can only rightly be occupied by God; and when God's love abides there, then we are both enabled and required to give away all else to our brothers and sisters in need.

BOLDNESS BEFORE GOD
1 John 3:18–24

3:18 **Little children, let us love, not in word or speech, but in truth and action.** [19] **And by this we will know that we are from the truth and will reassure our hearts before him** [20] **whenever our hearts condemn us; for God is greater than our hearts, and he knows everything.** [21] **Beloved, if our hearts do not condemn us, we have boldness before God;** [22] **and we receive from him whatever we ask, because we obey his commandments and do what pleases him.**

[23] **And this is his commandment, that we should believe in the name of his Son Jesus Christ and love one another, just as he has commanded us.** [24] **All who obey his commandments abide in him, and he abides in them. And by this we know that he abides in us, by the Spirit that he has given us.**

This passage is not so much a carefully structured, unified section of the text as it is a series of small units held together by verbal repetition. Indeed, verse 18 is so much a transitional sentence that it could easily be considered part of the preceding passage, continuing the theme of love in action. "Truth" forms the bridge from verse 18 to verses 19–22, which center around confidence in our relationship with God. This confidence is based on the keeping of God's commandments, a theme which is then picked up in verses 23–24. Those verses, in turn, form a transition to chapters 4 and 5 (especially 4:1–18), establishing the themes of belief in Jesus, love for one another, mutual abiding between Christians and God, and the gift of the Spirit.

In relation to the preceding passage, 3:18 sums up the concern that love be a matter of concrete deeds, using a contrast between "word" and "action" that was commonplace in Greek philosophy. Of course, "truth" in the Gospel and letters of John can mean more than just "physical reality." In fact, it can mean something so much deeper as to be almost the opposite: the reality of God, the divine reality that underlies and sometimes overrules the reality of the visible world. It is from this reality that Christian acts of love emerge, not simply out of human affection and compassion (as important as these are), but out of the divine love that is the very nature of the God who created the universe and redeemed the human race. Christians belong to this reality; they are "from the truth" (v. 19). This expression (just as "from the Father" and "from the world" in 2:16 and 4:5, "belong to us" in 2:19, and "from God" in 3:10 and 4:1–7) signifies both origin and belonging. To be "from" the truth means to have come from the truth, to be part of the realm of truth, to have what pertains to the truth as a defining characteristic. Because "truth" in this sense means the reality of God, and the reality of God is love (4:8, 16), Christians who practice love in action and in truth can be sure that they do indeed belong to the truth of God.

That much is clear about the meaning of verses 19–20. On the whole, however, these verses present an extraordinary tangle of grammar and vocabulary in the Greek. The issues have to do with whether the verb in the second half of verse 19 means "convince" or "reassure"; whether the conjunction at the beginning of verse 20 means "that," "for," or "whenever"; and whether that same conjunction, repeated later in verse 20, means "for" or is simply redundant. The easiest way of grasping the ambiguities and the various possibilities of translation may be to compare several different versions that represent different ways of solving the problems. The New Revised Standard Version, printed above, essentially agrees with the Revised Standard Version and the *New International Version*. The King James Version represents a different understanding, and the *New English Bible* yet another. On the whole, the NEB's translation seems to me to represent the least stretching of words to mean what they do not normally mean, even though it requires assuming that the author used an extra conjunction in verse 20 that adds nothing to the sense (as in colloquial English we sometimes say, "I told her that if she wrote to me that I would write back"). I would translate verses 19 and 20 as follows: "And by this we will know that we are from the truth and will convince our hearts before him that, if our hearts condemn us, God is greater than our hearts and knows everything."

What does this sentence, translated in this way, mean? It is evidently intended to be reassuring, but because of its ambiguous and unclear construction, most commentators before the modern period considered it to be a stern warning of divine judgment! In fact, however, the general tone of 1 John is one of reassurance (2:1–2, 17; 2:28–3:2; 4:17–18). Elsewhere in the Bible, the idea that God knows everything can be a threat (Ps. 7:9; Prov. 15:3, 11; Jer. 20:12; Heb. 4:12–13), but it can also be a promise of right judgment (1 Sam. 16:7; 1 Chron. 28:9; Acts 1:24–25; 15:8; 1 Cor. 4:5; note also John 21:17). Here the idea is that God, who knows everything, knows that we are "from the truth." We, however, may need a little reminder, especially when our consciences are troubling us. If it gets to the point that we wonder whether we belong to God at all, then 1 John suggests there is nothing wrong with remembering some of the good we have done for others. These deeds of love are the surest sign that we do in fact belong to God, and have not irreparably broken the relationship. God is greater than our heart: greater, that is, than our own tender consciences, and even greater than what our hearts believe possible for God. Before the incredible depth and breadth of divine compassion and forgiveness, we must bow in profound gratitude, pick ourselves up, and walk on, knowing that by God's mercy we are still walking in the light.

Verses 21–22 may present the alternative to this, the times when our consciences are clear. On the other hand, they might present the *outcome* of verses 19–20, for once we have convinced our hearts that God knows we are "from the truth," they no longer condemn us. In either case, the same reasoning prevails. Having kept the commandment of love, we are in a solid relationship with God (even if we sometimes need a bit of persuading about this ourselves), and we can feel confident when we go to God in prayer. All the Gospels include Jesus' teaching about asking God for something with the expectation of receiving it (Matt. 7:7–8; Mark 11:24; Luke 11:9–10; John 16:23–27). None of them, however (not even John 15:7–17), makes quite such a direct connection between obedience and reward as these verses seem to suggest. Many of us, indeed, will find it hard to verify that "we receive from him whatever we ask, because we obey his commandments." Everyone who prays knows the experience of high hopes that are dashed or desperate pleas that go unfulfilled. Does this passage suggest that if we pray and do not receive what we want, we must somehow have disobeyed a divine commandment; that if only we were better Christians our lives would go well and we would get everything we want? We occasionally encounter such teachings, but they seem to me far removed from the New Testament conception of Christian life.

There are several factors to consider. First of all, Jesus, the Gospel writers, and Paul (Phil. 4:6), as well as 1 John, do teach that God hears prayer and that those who pray receive what they request. The opposite side of the coin from the universal experience of unanswered prayer is the universal experience of answers to prayer, and sometimes quite unexpected ones. To ask with the expectation of receiving is part of that sense of confidence in God that Jesus and the earliest Christian writers call "faith." Faith, in this sense, is not a doctrinal conviction or a "belief system," but *trust*, a reliance on God as pure and expectant as the reliance of children on their mothers and fathers. It is part of a real relationship with God, lively and capable of growth, like our relationships with parents, spouses, and friends. In any such relationship there are highs and lows, of course, and it may be only in rare moments that we experience a truly clear and untroubled faith. But faith, in this sense of reliance on God, is the atmosphere in which confident prayer lives.

It is in this context of intimate acquaintance with God that the language of obedience in relation to prayer must be understood. In this relationship, where there is a genuine knowledge of God (see comments on 1 John 2:3), we can develop a greater understanding of God's will and a greater commitment to it. This growth in relationship with God not only produces deeper obedience, but also affects what we are likely to pray for! Our definition of what we want from God, and even of what we need, may change. In this sense, it may be profoundly true that "we receive what we ask, because we obey God's commandments." Living in this kind of faithfulness to God has nothing to do with mechanically or ritualistically or legalistically obeying a list of rules. It means hearing God's will day by day, and seeking to live a life that is in conformity with the divine love that speaks to us. Such a life is by no means one of uninterrupted comfort and self-satisfaction. Paul speaks of learning to "rely not on ourselves but on God who raises the dead" (2 Cor. 1:9), and of living "as sorrowful, yet always rejoicing; as poor, yet making many rich; as having nothing, and yet possessing everything" (2 Cor. 6:10). Genuine faith in God, real reliance on God, means giving up the "world's" forms of security. We can trust in

God or we can trust in our savings accounts, our reputations, our talent, our hard work, our achievements; we cannot serve two masters. When Jesus' disciples were sent out without money or bag (Mark 6:8), what would it have meant for them to pray, "Give us this day our daily bread"?

The factors I have discussed may not solve every problem regarding 1 John's expectation that we will "receive whatever we ask." However, I hope that this discussion will at least clarify the mindset behind this expectation. The expectation arises out of a deep and living relationship with God, a relationship of faith, a decision to turn aside from other sources of security in order to count on God, to run the risk of truly trusting in God.

We may note in passing that 1 John, in contrast to the Gospel of John, does not speak of praying to Jesus or in the name of Jesus (John 14:13–14; 15:7, 16; 16:23–27). Likewise, in the following verses Christians abide directly in God (and vice versa), rather than abiding in Jesus who abides in God (John 14:20; 15:4–10; 17:21–23); and it is God who gives the commandments that they keep, rather than Jesus (John 14:15–24). Despite the author's strong insistence on the importance of right belief in Jesus as the means to abiding in God, he seems to prefer speaking of the direct relationship of Christians to God, rather than of Jesus as the permanent mediator between them (though see 1 John 2:1). In the context here, this may be because he is speaking of Christians as keeping God's commandments and always doing what pleases God, who therefore listens to them. In the Gospel of John, these same things are said about Jesus himself (John 8:29, 55; 10:17–18; 11:22, 42; 12:49–50; 14:30–31; 15:10–13). Thus Christians, in their relationship with God, including obedience and prayer, are once again imitators of Jesus.

Verses 23–24, the transition to the following passages, set up the themes that those passages will treat, including the theme of mutual abiding between Christians and God, and the theme of the Spirit. Obviously both this abiding and the gift of the Spirit are individual and interior phenomena, taking place within each believer's heart. Yet we find in the following passages that both are validated by means that are quite public. Those who claim to speak by the Spirit must rightly confess Jesus as the Christ (the first commandment here); those who would abide in God and have God abiding in them must love one another (the second commandment). Both of these are actions that take place within a community of faith, not in individual isolation. Indeed, tests for whether one authentically abides in God (and vice versa) have already been named in 1 John 2:5–6, 24 and 3:6; and these tests also involve belief in Jesus and living in love. Thus these very *personal* matters of relationship with God are not allowed to remain *private;* they are authenticated in the open life of the Christian community.

These verses are more than just a transitional unit, however. The author is clearly stating here what he believes to be essential Christianity. He does so in terms of "commandments," a factor that will be considered below. For now, we may note that he first speaks of commandments in verse 22; then of a single commandment at the beginning of verse 23, and again at the end of that verse (which may be more literally translated, "just as he has given us a commandment"); then of commandments in the plural again in verse 24. It seems likely that the plurals refer to the two commandments taken together, and each singular "commandment" to one of the specific commandments, belief and love, respectively. At any rate, it is clear that 1 John is not speaking of a long list of commandments, not even of ten commandments, but of just these two, which are considered in such close association that neither can be fully separated from the other.

One of these commandments speaks of our relationship to the divine, the other of our relationship to other people. They thus run parallel to the two commandments singled out as the greatest by Jesus, according to Mark 12:28–34. On the other hand, their understanding of what God requires is very much characteristic of the type of Christianity represented by the Gospel and letters of John. The first commandment is, not to love God, but to believe in Jesus. Indeed, the terms in which this commandment is phrased, "that we should believe in the name of his Son Jesus Christ," repeat almost exactly those of John 20:31, which states the aim that the Fourth Gospel seeks to achieve. (On the significance of Jesus' "name," see the comments on 1 John 2:12.) The author is appealing to the history of the Christian community from which this Gospel and these letters emerged, interpreting that community's faithfulness to the confession of Jesus as Messiah and Son of God as faithfulness to God's commandment. By implication, the opponents, who in some way separated or distinguished the human Jesus from the divine Christ and placed little value on the former, would be betraying both this tradition and the divine commandment that it represents. As for the second commandment here, it is phrased not in terms of love for one's neighbor in general but in terms of love for "one another." This is the distinctive form of the commandment of love in the Gospel of John (13:34–35; 15:12, 17). It also reflects the history of this community, which, under the pressure of persecution, seems to have looked inward much more than outward in its love relationships (see comments on 1 John 2:10). This commandment, too, may have been neglected by the author's opponents, who may have given scant attention to human relations in general in favor of a one-sided emphasis on the divine, and who may not have considered the loving sacrifice of the human Jesus significant either for salvation or for ethical imitation.

Looking to the history and the tradition of his community, the author of 1 John sees two things, belief in the human Jesus as divine Christ and Son of God and love for one another, as the central and indispensable elements of Christian existence. Indeed, he says that these two things are commandments, something that God requires of those who would be obedient. What do we make of this? How can anyone, even God, *command* us what to believe and what to feel? We may try to obey, and say that we believe, and call what we feel "love"; but in the end, our hearts and our minds are free, and they can only think and feel what they genuinely think and feel.

As for belief, we can sense here (and indeed already in the Gospel of John, for example 8:24) the beginnings of Christian dogmatism, by which I mean a demand that people believe certain formulas, accept certain particularly worded statements of faith, in order to be in right relationship with God. Different Christian denominations have taken different approaches to this matter, and for some, dogmatic belief is seen as a necessary means of ensuring the unity of the church and the preservation of the truth. Clearly our author felt this way. The danger in such an approach is that faith, in the sense of a living relationship with God, as discussed above, can give way to a mere mechanical mental assent: sign on the dotted line and you are saved. Does 1 John fall into this trap? We should remember that this text was written in response to a particular situation, in which not the form but the content of belief in Jesus was being challenged. It is this content that is the issue for 1 John (and 2 John). The author does not specify an exact formula of words, or set out a fully developed system of doctrine, or even seem to think that such a system is possible or necessary. His required creed remains very simple; yet there can be no mistaking that that is what it is. To be in relationship with God, one must know where God is to be encountered. For 1 John, that means recognizing the revelation that God has made in Jesus Christ, both fully human and the fully divine Son of God.

As for the second commandment, perhaps what really matters is not that love is made into a commandment, but that the commandment is *love*. According to 1 John, what God requires is not ritual purity, nor perfect adherence to a detailed moral code, nor maintaining the traditional values of society intact and unchanged. It is simply love for one another. Every act of love is a means of obeying this commandment of God, whether or not it is part of a religious, moral, or social canon of behavior. Concerning such things there is no law, as Galatians 5:23 has it (according to one understanding). Moreover, as noted in the comments on the preceding passage, 1 John, like the New Testament generally, does not think of love primarily in terms of feeling, but in terms of action. We are not commanded to feel love but to act lovingly. To be sure, acting contrary to one's feelings can produce a great deal of unacknowledged anger. Yet on the other hand, gentle actions can also soften the emotions. Persistently acting in love is one way of guiding the heart toward feelings of love as well. Whether or not our author is thinking in such terms, he understands the commandment to love one another not as an arbitrary demand picked out of the air, but as part of the Christian gospel, the good news that God is love and has opened up the way of love to all who will accept it (on this point also, see the comments on 1 John 3:11–17). Those who love their brothers and sisters are acting in accordance with the very nature of God. For that reason they can be assured that they abide in God and God in them.

These two commandments—to believe in Jesus and to love one another—mean accepting God's self-revelation as love, a revelation made in the One who lovingly laid down his life for us. The Spirit may lead Christians into new truth, but it will never overturn this truth, as the author believes his opponents have done. Though the commandments are two, there is an essential unity to them; neither one is viable without the other. No one can really accept God's revelation in Jesus Christ without also setting out to walk in the way that Jesus walked, the way of love displayed in concrete actions. Yet this love is more than the ordinary warmth and tenderness of everyday life. It is the utterly self-giving love that lies at the center of the universe, the love that God is, fully made known and made available to us in Jesus, the Messiah and Son of God.

BELIEVING AND LOVING
1 John 4:1–18

In this unit of the text, the two commandments and the other themes established in the preceding passage (3:23–24) are considered in more detail in two separate but related passages. In 4:1–6, the commandment of believing in Jesus is treated in relation to those who claim to speak under the influence of the Spirit but do not make the true confession of Jesus. In 4:7–18, the commandment of loving one another is given a carefully structured exposition in relation to God's love for us and God's abiding in us.

The Spirit is mentioned again, and there is further discussion of God's sending of Jesus and our confession of him. Thus the two passages are brought into relation to one another, as are the two commandments.

The Spirit of Truth and the Spirit of Error (4:1–6)

4:1 **Beloved, do not believe every spirit, but test the spirits to see whether they are from God; for many false prophets have gone out into the world. ² By this you know the Spirit of God: every spirit that confesses that Jesus Christ has come in the flesh is from God, ³ and every spirit that does not confess Jesus is not from God. And this is the spirit of the antichrist, of which you have heard that it is coming; and now it is already in the world. ⁴ Little children, you are from God, and have conquered them; for the one who is in you is greater than the one who is in the world. ⁵ They are from the world; therefore what they say is from the world, and the world listens to them. ⁶ We are from God. Whoever knows God listens to us, and whoever is not from God does not listen to us. From this we know the spirit of truth and the spirit of error.**

This passage divides easily into two short units, the first treating the Spirit of God and the spirit of antichrist (vv. 1–3), and the second analogously treating people who are of God and people who are of the world (vv. 4–6). Verse 6 ends with a reference to the spirits of truth and error, neatly rounding off the passage.

Having just cited the Spirit as a sign of God's abiding in Christian believers, the author must now give a warning that not everything that seems to represent the Spirit of God really does so. In the early decades of the church, and indeed well into the second century, the inspiration of the Holy Spirit played an important and sometimes controversial role in Christian congregations. It is commonly said that as reliance on the direct work of the Spirit became less of a factor in the church the role of institutional structures became greater. This is obviously true; but at the same time those institutional structures have also claimed the guidance of the Spirit. Moreover, renewal movements of various sorts have reasserted the importance of the gifts of the Spirit throughout Christian history, from the Montanists of the second century, through the various spiritual awakenings in twelfth and thirteenth century Europe and some of the more radical groups in the Protestant Reformation, down to the modern charismatic movements inside and outside established denominations. A number of these movements were declared heretical; others have managed to find some acceptance and to demonstrate doctrinal orthodoxy. What we find in 1 John is one of the earliest records of conflict over claims to the inspiration of the Spirit.

People claiming to act under the influence of the Holy Spirit played a number of roles in the earliest years of the church. They led missionary work and performed miracles, spoke in tongues and interpreted such speech, taught and exhorted the congregations, uttered prophecies and produced "spiritual songs" (Acts 2:1–41; 4:8–12; 6:1–10; 11:27–28; 13:1–4; 15:32; 16:6–10; 19:1–7; 21:8–11; 1 Cor. 7:40; 12:1–14:40; Eph. 5:18–20; Col. 3:16). Indeed, the Pauline letters seem to consider every role of leadership or service performed in the church to be a gift of the Spirit (Rom. 12:4–8; 1 Cor. 12:1–11, 28–31; Eph. 4:7–13). Some of these activities were no doubt similar to those considered "ecstatic" or "charismatic" today; others may have been less obviously the product of spiritual rapture, but were also considered to be the result of divine inspiration. In the tradition represented by the Gospel and letters of John, the Spirit was most closely associated with teaching (John 14:26; 16:13; this is the role of the "anointing" in 1 John 2:20, 27). It would not have mattered whether such teachers seemed to be in an ecstatic or trance-like state; teaching itself was considered "charismatic," the work of the Holy Spirit, in this community.

We should never underestimate the role that such spiritual experience played in the life of the early Christian churches. As is often the case in new religious movements (including new movements within Christianity), a vivid sense of the presence of God's Spirit was an important factor in the growth, development, and life of the church. When the Gospel of John portrays Jesus as quoting from the prophets, "And they shall all be taught by God" (John 6:45), it represents the Christian community's conviction that their belief in Jesus and their new ideas were directly given to them by the divine Spirit (note also John 20:22–23). Take note sometime of all the references to joy and rejoicing in Acts and the letters of Paul. We may be quite certain that all this exuberance was not because the worship service got finished by noon! Many of the New Testament writings attest a glad sense of divine intervention and divine presence in the life of the church and the lives of Christians, and much of this intervention was attributed to the Holy Spirit.

Claims to be a teacher, healer, or prophet inspired by the Spirit could produce controversy, however. Not everyone accepted all of these claims. Even Paul recommends weighing and testing the words of prophets (1 Cor. 14:29; 1 Thess. 5:20–22). We find a surprising number of references to false prophets, messiahs, apostles, and teachers (Matt. 24:11; Mark 13:5–6, 21–22; 2 Cor. 11:13; 1 Tim. 4:1; 2 Peter 2:1; Rev. 2:2, 20;

12:9; 13:11–15; 16:13–14; 19:20; 20:10). A number of early Christian writings propose tests to validate claims to the Spirit. Within the New Testament, Matthew 7:15–23 insists on righteous conduct for those who claim
to do supernatural deeds in Jesus' name (note also 1 Cor. 12:3). The early
writing called the *Didache* proposes both tests of conduct and doctrinal
tests for prophets and teachers (chap. 11). This passage in 1 John, which
also proposes a doctrinal criterion, fits quite well into this tradition of testing prophets, a tradition that may originate with Deuteronomy 13:1–5 and
18:20–22. The main test in Deuteronomy is whether would-be prophets
speak in the name of previously unknown gods. It is in accord with this that
1 John associates its opponents with idols (5:21) and opposes them by appealing to the teaching about Jesus that has been known "from the beginning."

Because teaching was considered the work of the Spirit in this community, it is not surprising that 1 John attacks those whom it considers to be
false teachers as false *prophets*. Moreover, since the rise of false prophets
was part of what was expected in the last days, it is also natural to find these
false prophets linked to "the antichrist" (see comments on 1 John 2:18).
They are also implicitly connected with the devil, who is likely meant by
"the one who is in the world" (4:4; compare 5:19). "The spirit of the
antichrist" then is probably also the devil, as the spirit who inspires these
"antichrist" teachers. On the other hand, the plurality of spirits in 4:1–3
may suggest that the author also thinks of various spirits inspiring the
opponents, under the direction of the evil one. The picture then is of people
claiming to give Christian teaching under the influence of the Holy Spirit.
The content of their teaching, however, leads our author to say that it fails
to conform to what the Spirit of truth would teach, and therefore must
come from "the spirit of error." As elsewhere in 1 John, there is no middle
ground; teaching comes either from the Spirit of God or from the devil.

The specific area of teaching that the author disputes concerns ideas
about Jesus. Here for the first time the author sets out directly what it is
that the opponents should teach but do not. Unfortunately, his tendency
toward unclear writing appears once again at this crucial moment. His formulation of the confession of Jesus that truly comes from the Spirit of God
is (to us at least) thoroughly ambiguous, though it is possible that his first
readers, who knew what everyone involved in the situation was saying,
could understand it clearly. Because this is the most direct statement in
1 John about the teaching that it opposes, our interpretation of this statement affects how we understand the document as a whole.

Translated literally, the Greek of verse 2 reads, "In this you know the
Spirit of God: every spirit that confesses Jesus Christ having come in flesh

is from God." The NRSV rendering "confesses that Jesus Christ has come in the flesh" seems quite adequate at first sight, but it is not the only possible translation. For one thing, the particular sentence construction used here would normally serve to lay emphasis on the *person* who has come, rather than on the bare fact *that* someone has come. Thus, there are several other translation possibilities. When we compare verse 2 with verse 3 and with some other, much clearer passages in 1 John (2:22; 4:15; 5:1, 5), we get the impression that the central issue is *the identity of Jesus:* he is to be confessed "as Christ who has come in the flesh." This would be a perfectly acceptable understanding of the Greek grammar, and would probably mean that the Jesus of human flesh is to be confessed as the divine Christ. However, the two words "Jesus" and "Christ," without the verb "is" between them, generally form a single proper name elsewhere in 1 John (1:3; 2:1; 3:23; 5:6, 20), and that is probably the case here as well. Indeed, 1 John 5:6 suggests that it is *the coming of Jesus Christ,* that is, his coming into the world to bring salvation, that is the issue. If so, then the best translation may be "confesses Jesus Christ as having come in flesh." That is, Jesus Christ, one single person, is to be confessed as having entered the world in physical human reality.

What does it mean that the opponents "did not confess Jesus" in this sense? It may be that they simply denied that Jesus Christ was really a mortal human being, seeing him instead as a purely spiritual entity. That would have made them full-fledged docetists (see the Introduction to 1 John for the significance of this). However, the problem may also have lain elsewhere. The passages noted above in relation to the *identity* of Jesus suggest that this was part of the issue. The opponents may have distinguished between Jesus, a physical human being, and the Christ, a spiritual divine being who "came" into the world to bring a purely spiritual salvation. The coming of this being, and the bringing of salvation, would thus not have been "in flesh." The Jesus of human flesh might be at most a temporary vehicle, a kind of carrier, but would have no significance in himself for salvation. The author of 1 John rejects this idea. For him, Jesus Christ, human being of flesh and divine Son of God, brought salvation into the world precisely "in flesh," in his physical human nature; for it was in his body that he made known the God who is love by sacrificing his mortal, fleshly life for us.

Remember that the grammar of verse 2 suggests that what must be confessed is not a statement of fact, but a person. It is Jesus Christ who is to be confessed, not a statement about him. People outside the Christian faith (and not a few people inside it!) often puzzle over the role that it ascribes to Jesus. The New Testament Gospels present him as a prophet and a teacher, which might make him the equivalent of Moses or Muhammad; and as a man deeply in touch with the divine, which could perhaps put him in a league with the Buddha. But Christianity persistently refuses to accept these categorizations and claims something utterly unique for Jesus. For this reason, Christianity itself is uniquely *about* Jesus. Judaism is about God and God's Torah; Islam is about obedience to Allah; Buddhism is about enlightenment. Christianity is about Jesus. Everything that it offers, including ethical obedience and spiritual enlightenment (not to mention eternal life) is mediated through him. To some people, this seems to be assigning too high a place to someone who was, after all, a man like others. But our claim is not simply that this man was God; it is that God became this man. The Creator of the universe sought out the human race in love, and came and encountered us, not in a law, a ritual, a text, or a philosophy, but in a human being. God met us in our own condition, and chose to do so in the man Jesus of Nazareth. Therefore it is this person, uniquely embodying both the highest of human spirituality and the fullness of the presence of God, who is at the center of Christianity.

For 1 John, the proper confession of this person is as "having come in flesh," having brought salvation precisely as a human being. That isn't much of a problem for most people today, who, as I just noted, readily acknowledge that Jesus was fully human. Perhaps for that very reason, though, some Christians show a kind of defensive tendency, wanting to safeguard the divinity of Jesus, but thereby putting his humanity in jeopardy. If a movie comes out that portrays Jesus as having sexual desires that cause him temptation, or if a theologian suggests that Jesus may have had some political intentions, there will be devout Christians who leap to the barricades. "No, no—how can you speak of Jesus as if he were a man?" With all due regard for their devotion to Jesus, Christian belief is precisely that he was a man, one "who in every respect has been tested as we are" (Heb. 4:15). If he genuinely entered into the reality of human life, then we cannot deny that he knew our temptations, and that he spoke to all of human life, including politics as well as "spiritual things." There may be nothing harder in Christian teaching than to maintain this balance, to accept this mystery. We cannot say, "He was not a man"; we cannot say, "He was only a man." Each of us will find different ways in which we lose the balance, and different ways in which we grasp the mystery. First John, for all the unclarity of its language at times, holds tightly to this unique confession of a person, Jesus Christ, the Son of God who came in the flesh.

It may be just as well that God did not take a poll, did not ask us what we were looking for in the way of a savior. We might have requested one who stood so far above us that he could not really know us. Christian faith has seen in Jesus someone who does know all our weakness, pain, and longing, and yet who brings to us a strength and a love that come from God. In the time and culture where Christianity began, however, there were many people who understood human beings as having a divine side that was simply oppressed by "the flesh," and who therefore would have expected a divine savior to be untouched by human limitations. Our author's opponents evidently followed this tendency. He says that they were "many" (2:18; 4:1) and that "what they say is from the world, and the world listens to them" (4:5). This suggests that they may have tried to shape their presentation of Christianity to fit the popular ideas of the time, and that they were having some success. In every place where the gospel has been preached, the question of how far to adapt it to the local culture has arisen. Inevitably, what some people see as necessary compromise, or even as objective truth (because of their own culturally limited vision), others see as betrayal and loss of the gospel's distinctiveness. Should women conform to cultural dress codes when addressing the congregation? Paul said yes, though he apparently got some flak for it (1 Cor. 11:2–16); a later letter written in his name takes cultural conformity even further and does not allow women to address the congregation at all (1 Tim. 2:11–12)! Should Jesus be presented as truly a man, or as a superhuman savior? First John's opponents may well have thought that they were simply expressing the truth of salvation in a way that made better sense for their Greek audience. Our author believed that they had abandoned the truth by abandoning the saving significance of Jesus' humanity, and thus had become mouthpieces of the antichrist and the world. Their numerical success was only the final proof of this.

Indeed, "the world" in some ways means precisely the surrounding culture to which the opponents evidently sought to adapt their message. As in 1 John 2:15–17; 3:1, 13; 5:4–5, 19, the world is set over against the Christian community, and specifically over against the author and his readers. The readers have conquered the world and the evil one (2:12–14); now they are said to have conquered "them," that is, the opponents, as well. "You are from God" and "We are from God." "We [the author and the readers] know the spirit of truth and the spirit of error," he writes, because "whoever knows God [the readers] listens to us [the author]" (4:4, 6). Either the author is quite confident that his audience really does already agree with him, or he is going out on a limb by speaking to them as if they do.

The spirit of truth and the spirit of error (4:6) clearly seem to be the same as the Spirit of God and the spirit of the antichrist in 4:2–3. "Spirit of truth" is a typical designation for the Holy Spirit in the Gospel and letters of John (John 14:17; 15:26; 16:13; note also 4:23–24; 1 John 2:27; 5:6). It is not found anywhere else in the New Testament, though it is found in the Dead Sea Scrolls and some other ancient Jewish writings. This is one of a number of indications that some of the ideas in this Gospel and letters may have originated among the more esoteric branches of ancient Judaism. As John and 1 John use it, "Spirit of truth" associates the Holy Spirit with the divine truth, the reality of God. Teaching that comes from this Spirit, then, will reflect that reality; it will not misrepresent or distort the nature of God or of God's Son. The expression "spirit of error" might be more clearly rendered "spirit of deceit." The elder does not think of the teaching it represents as merely mistaken, but as deceptive and likely to lead people astray (1 John 1:8; 2:26; 3:7).

Once again the author presents himself and those who agree with him as on the side of God, and his opponents as on the side of the world and the devil. Such sharp distinctions and strong attacks were common in the thinking and the rhetoric of that time. Like the use of the term "antichrist" to describe the opponents, however, their effect on Christian history has not always been a happy one. All too readily the picture of a cosmic struggle between the forces of God and the forces of Satan has been imported into conflicts among Christians, so that simple disagreement and honest debate become difficult if not impossible. Claiming that your opponent is a tool of the devil means that it is no longer possible to consider what he or she says thoughtfully; there is no chance that any portion of their reasoning could be correct or worthwhile, or that they could have any good intention of faithfulness to Christ. First John's legacy of uncompromising insistence on maintaining the balance between humanity and divinity in our understanding of Jesus Christ is something for which Christian readers today can and should be grateful. Its legacy of demonizing one's opponents in disputes within the church, however, is much more questionable.

God Is Love (4:7–18)

4:7 **Beloved, let us love one another, because love is from God; everyone who loves is born of God and knows God. [8] Whoever does not love does not know God, for God is love. [9] God's love was revealed among us in this way: God sent his only Son into the world so that we might live through him. [10] In this is love, not that we loved God but that he loved us and sent his Son to be the atoning** sacrifice for our sins. ¹¹ Beloved, since God loved us so much, we also ought to love one another. ¹² No one has ever seen God; if we love one another, God lives in us, and his love is perfected in us.

¹³ By this we know that we abide in him and he in us, because he has given us of his Spirit. ¹⁴ And we have seen and do testify that the Father has sent his Son as the Savior of the world. ¹⁵ God abides in those who confess that Jesus is the Son of God, and they abide in God. ¹⁶ So we have known and believe the love that God has for us.

God is love, and those who abide in love abide in God, and God abides in them. ¹⁷ Love has been perfected among us in this: that we may have boldness on the day of judgment, because as he is, so are we in this world. ¹⁸ There is no fear in love, but perfect love casts out fear; for fear has to do with punishment, and whoever fears has not reached perfection in love.

Now we turn to the second of the two commandments listed in 1 John 3:23, the commandment to love one another. The NRSV translation, shown above, represents one very common way of understanding the structure of this passage. It is not the only possible understanding, however. The theme of imitation, that Christians should love because of God's love, appears in verses 7, 11, and 19; and verses 7 and 11 each begin by addressing the readers ("Beloved . . ."). This suggests that these verses mark the beginnings of new sections in the text. Verses 7–10 focus on the nature of God as love, and how this love was revealed in the sending of Jesus. Verses 11–18 have a more complex and subtle structure. After the opening of the section in verse 11, verse 12 provides a double thematic statement: God abides in us (NRSV "lives in us"), and God's love is perfected in us. These two topics are then unfolded in the rest of the passage: verses 13–16 treat God's abiding in us, and verses 17–18 treat the perfection of divine love. Within the discussion of abiding in verses 13–16, we may discern a further structure with three parts, setting out three things that fulfill the opening statement, "By this we know that we abide in him and he in us." These three things are the *Spirit*, right *confession of Jesus*, and *love*. Those who have the Spirit, confess Jesus, and love one another can be certain that they abide in God and God in them. It is even possible to find a progression in thought among these three "criteria" for divine indwelling. Having the Spirit indicated this indwelling in 3:24; but according to 4:1–3, having the Spirit of God must be demonstrated by right confession of Jesus. According to 4:9–10, moreover, Jesus was sent by God to reveal divine love. Therefore the confession in verses 14–15 is framed in terms of the "sending" of Jesus, leading to the reminder of divine love in verse 16. Thus the abiding of God is signalled by the Spirit, but the Spirit must be confirmed by right confession, and the outcome of confession has to be love. By repeating that "God is love" and that we should imitate that love, verse 16 rounds off this entire movement of thought, which incorporates all the major ideas since 3:23, and forms as much of a climax as 1 John has. All in all, the structure of the present passage is probably the best conceived and the best executed in this book. As a good literary structure should do, it helps the reader to follow the author's thought clearly and enjoyably.

Though this passage elaborates on the second commandment in 3:23, it speaks of love not in terms of a commandment but in terms of the very nature of God. The people who are "born of God" and are "from God" (2:29; 3:9–10; 4:1–6) should act in ways that accord with what God is. One of the major themes in 1 John is that relationship with God is seen and demonstrated in how people relate to one another. Here we see the ultimate basis for that claim: God is love, something that can only exist as a relationship. The statement that "God is love" is found only in 1 John in the entire Bible, though in the New Testament it has roots in Jesus' message of God's mercy and love as the fundamental means of obedience to God, and in the Hebrew Scriptures God's love, especially God's steadfast covenant love, is the reason for the choosing of Israel (for example, 1 Kings 8:23; Pss. 98:3; 130:7; 136; Isa. 63:7–9; Hos. 11:1). Perhaps it is from traditions such as these that our author has drawn his sweeping conclusion.

The assertion that God is love has to do not with the essence of divine *being* as a matter of abstract theological speculation but with what God *does.* Love is an activity, not a quality, and saying that God is love suggests an active and dynamic God, not a remote, "hands-off" deity or a static intellectual concept. Moreover, since love cannot really exist without an object, the claim that God is love also provides a Christian theological starting point for understanding the nature of God as Trinity (the oneness of God expressed in three Persons who exist in mutual love) and the creation of the world (so that God's love might have an object). These implications go well beyond what 1 John is interested in, however. Our author speaks of God as love in order to present a model for Christians to imitate. We cannot be what God is, but we can do as God does. Patterning our actions after the love of God, the love that God is, provides the clearest indication that we are genuinely in relationship with God, that we are God's children and know God. In and of itself, the statement that "everyone who loves is born of God and knows God" has a very broad scope. It seems to claim that everyone who acts lovingly—even those who do not believe in God!—knows God. But again, that would take us beyond the author's frame of reference. In its context here, the statement is intended to let the readers know how to tell who *in their fragmented Christian community* really is in relationship with God. The opponents, with their lack of concern for the human needs of their brothers and sisters, disqualify themselves, despite what they may say. If they do not love, they do not know God; and so once again, they are aligned with "the world" (3:1; 4:5).

Indeed, 1 John's understanding of how love was revealed makes it clear that the author is only concerned with ideas and actions within the circle of Christianity. God's love was made known to us in the sending of Jesus Christ, and it is those who acknowledge this sending who can acknowledge that God is love (4:9–10, 14–16). The sending of the Son of God revealed that God is love, and it revealed the nature of that love: God's Son came and gave up his own life so that we might live (compare John 3:16; on the term "atoning sacrifice," see the comments on 1 John 2:2). Love is thus defined as the giving up of one's own self-interest for the sake of one's beloved, not only a *feeling* of affection and concern, but an *action* of self-giving. This is not an elaborate definition of what love is and does, not even as elaborate as Paul's discussion in 1 Corinthians 13. Yet it is enough (along with 1 John 3:16–17) to show the basic course that love—God's love—will take. It is then up to us to explore that course, to follow actively in the path that Christ has opened, to "walk just as he walked" (2:6).

The idea that God "sent" Jesus is one of the most characteristic themes of the Gospel of John (see, for example, not only John 3:16, but also 5:23–24, 36–38; 7:16–18, 28–29; 17:3, 18–25). That Gospel also speaks of Jesus revealing God, making God known, so that those who have seen Jesus have seen God (John 1:18; 8:19; 14:7–11). By appealing to these ideas in this context, our author gives us another reminder that a true understanding of Jesus and a true Christian ethical life—the two commandments of 3:23—are inseparable. Jesus' humanity was not irrelevant to the fact that God sent him to bring life and divine revelation. Rather, it was precisely by means of his humanity—by means of his very human death—that he gave life and made God known; for it was in his death that God was revealed as love. Having received this life and this revelation, we, in turn, are bound to shape our own humanity after that of Jesus. If what he did with his human life made God known to us as *love*, then what we do with our human lives will show whether or not we have truly taken in this revelation, for love is something that a human life can embody.

The claim that God is love seems one-sided when we look at all that is said about God in the Bible, including references to divine wrath and the final judgment, not only in the Old Testament but also in the New. Yet this only serves to highlight the fact that 1 John, for all its harsh language about the opponents, is remarkably free of angry, judgmental images of God. God's righteousness is connected with forgiveness, not punishment (1:9), just as the righteousness of God's children is connected with love (3:10). It is, in fact, divine love that has made us children of God and will make us to be like God (3:1–2); and this same love means that we need have no fear of the day of judgment (4:17–18, to be discussed shortly). The fact that God knows all about us is something that we can use to encourage ourselves when our own consciences condemn us (3:19–20). Indeed, it is God who has taken the initiative in love (4:10, 19); mercy was shown to us before we could even ask, and the result for us is eternal life (4:9; 5:11–13). First John's understanding of God may be one-sided, but it seems to be an understanding that has been deliberately chosen and consistently portrayed. God is not pictured as a wrathful judge, a nitpicking accountant, or an avenger lying in wait. Rather, God is represented as generous, self-giving, and compassionate; in a word: God is love.

Because it is God who has taken the initiative in love, our own love for one another is a result of our relationship with God, not the cause of it. We are born of God, and so, like God, we love. Yet 1 John also seems to say that love is the way to know God, suggesting that our knowledge of God—our relationship with God—is the result of our love after all. So which comes first, our love for one another or our relationship with God? Such questions of priority and sequence may be of interest to us, but they take us beyond where 1 John is interested in going. Indeed, they risk overlooking what is most fundamental about 1 John's understanding of relationship with God. This relationship is a gift of God's love, a love revealed in Jesus the Son of God; but the relationship itself consists in loving one another. We only accept the revelation in Jesus, and the relationship with God that comes with it, when we ourselves act in love. Indeed, our love for one another is fundamental to this relationship with God; without our love, the relationship that God initiated does not exist. God loved us first; but divine love leaves no trace unless there is human love to correspond to it.

First John 4:11–18 begins by summing up the thought of verses 7–10 in terms of the imitation of God (see the comments on 1 John 2:28–3:10). The structure of this exhortation to love one another was discussed at the beginning of the comments on this passage. Verse 12 provides a heading that introduces the themes of abiding in God and the perfection of love. It begins, however, with a familiar idea that may seem somewhat out of place here. This is the idea, commonplace in Jewish theology and in the Christian theology based on it, that God cannot be seen. The classic statement of this idea in the Hebrew Bible is Exodus 33:19–23. First John, brief as it is, mentions seeing God twice elsewhere (3:2; 4:20). But why does it come up here? The Gospel of John makes the exact same statement (1:18), but goes on to say that God was made known by "the only Son" (very much as verse 9 here says that God's love was revealed by the sending of "his only Son"). This suggests a way of understanding verse 12. It must mean to indicate how God, whom no one has ever seen, has nevertheless been made known. The statement that God abides in those who love one another is a statement about how God is seen: God abides in them, and is seen and made known not only *to* them, but also *through* them to the world. Christian love for one another is the ongoing revelation of God; it is one of the ways in which the Christian community makes God known (compare John 13:35). Because God is love, our love is a manifestation of God. If the opponents, in their practice of mission, sought to adapt the Christian message to the spiritual preferences of their time by downplaying the humanity of Jesus (see the comments on the preceding passage), 1 John by contrast suggests that an essential part of Christian mission is the practice of love for one another. Since Jesus showed that a human life could disclose the nature of God, it is up to us, if we wish to demonstrate the reality of God, to do the same in our lives. This is another sense in which love is not law but gospel for 1 John (see comments on 3:11).

Verse 12 also says that God's love "is perfected in us" if we love one another. How can that be? Was God's love ever less than perfect? "Perfected" and the related words here and in 1 John 2:5 and 4:17–18 translate a verb that means "to complete, bring to the goal" (compare John 4:34; 5:36; 17:4; 19:28–30). It does not refer to flawlessness, but to completeness. The idea is thus that in Christian love for one another, divine love reaches its goal. When we love one another, God's love accomplishes what it set out to do; it is not finished without our love. Not only does our love reveal God, then, but in it the ultimate aims of creation and redemption are achieved. The world looks at a genuine example of Christian love and says, "That's it! That's what we were looking for! That's God!" God looks and says, "That's it! That's what I had in mind! Now it's done!" What greater incentive could there be to love one another?

In discussing the structure of verses 13–16 above, I suggested that the three criteria for mutual abiding with God that these verses set out show a progression of thought that sums up what the author has been saying since 3:23–24. The latter verses declare that believing in Jesus and loving one another lead to this mutual abiding, which is attested by the presence of the Spirit (on the subject of Christians abiding directly in God, see the comments on those verses). Here in 4:13–16, abiding is confirmed successively by the Spirit, confession of Jesus, and love. Moreover, 4:1–3 has shown that the genuine presence of the Spirit must be confirmed by right confession, and 4:9–10 has stated that confession of Jesus as the Son of God is tantamount to acknowledging that God is love, which then entails our love for one another. Thus all these evidences of true communion with God, of inner relationship with God, are deeply interrelated, and have their climax in love, since love is God's own nature. There is nothing more intimate, more personal, in human life than relationship with God, where our own deepest and most individual reality meets the reality that loved us and brought us into being. Yet 1 John insists that this most utterly interior and private phenomenon receives its true validation in the public and outward practices of love and confession of Jesus.

The concept of a personal religion that has no relation to the outward facts of our lives, of a private spirituality that has no bearing on our conduct toward other people, is as remote as it could possibly be from this author's understanding of what it means to abide in God and have God abiding in us. Modern Western society has tended toward an extreme individualism, and religion (or spirituality, if you prefer) has also tended to become highly privatized. As Stephen Carter observes in his book *The Culture of Disbelief*, public policy, the media, and even many religious people themselves have come to treat faith as a kind of hobby, one of many purely personal diversions that we have available to us. Carter calls for the return of religion, as the foundation of the believer's human life, to the public square. I think our author would agree. Confess and love in public, he says, or your meditation in private amounts to nothing.

Indeed, the author says that we not only confess but *testify* that God has sent Jesus as Savior of the world. The testimony is to what we have seen, that is, to the humanity of Jesus (1:1–3; John 1:34; 3:11, 32; 19:35), which is also where the unseen God has been revealed. "Savior of the world" is a title found only here and at John 4:42 in the New Testament. "Savior" was a title applied in the ancient world to gods and emperors. In the New Testament, it is used mainly for Jesus as Savior of God's people, whether Israel or Christians (see, for example, Luke 2:11; Acts 13:23; Eph. 5:23; 2 Tim. 1:10; Titus 3:4–6; 2 Peter 1:1, 11). The expression here reminds us that, for all its hostility toward "the world," that is, toward the human system that opposes God (2:15–17; 3:1, 13; 4:4–5; 5:4–5, 19), 1 John still regards the world as the object of God's love and seems to hold open the possibility of salvation for those who will transfer their allegiance from "the world" to the Son of God who is its Savior. For the present, however, it is those who believe who can say that they know God's love "for us" (v. 16)—or rather, "in us" or "among us" (as in v. 9), that is, in the midst of the community that shows by the mutual love within it that it has received the revelation of God in Jesus. The divine love revealed in Jesus is still the love that "God has in us" as we love one another.

Verse 12 introduced the theme of perfected love as well as the theme of God's abiding in us. Now, following the masterly treatment of divine abiding in verses 13–16, the author turns to perfect love in verses 17–18. Verse 12 had stated that God's love reaches perfection in us—that is, achieves its intended goal—when we love one another. Now we learn that the substance of this completed love is our confidence at the Last Judgment. In 2:28–3:3, the author spoke of such confidence as the result of "abiding in him" (probably meaning "in Jesus"), but quickly went on to mention being righteous like Jesus; and spoke further of an ultimate transformation into the likeness of God, a hope that should lead us to make ourselves pure as Jesus is pure. This theme of the imitation of Jesus recurs here: our confidence at the Judgment is due to our being like Jesus in this world. In essence, this is simply a restatement of verse 12, because to be like Jesus is to love one another, following the example of love that he set (2:6–11; 3:16); and in loving one another, we have God abiding in us, which is also a way of being like Jesus (John 10:38; 14:10–11, 20; 17:21–23). We imitate Jesus by loving one another, and thus God abides in us, as in Jesus; and the outcome is confidence at the Last Judgment, knowing that our likeness to Jesus *now* will result in a likeness to God *then*. Despite the reference to judgment, the author does not speak in terms of reward and punishment, but of likeness. Indeed, he rejects the fear of punishment as inappropriate for those who are like Jesus in their love. The Christian life in this world is not, for 1 John, one of stacking up achievements or building up positive entries in a heavenly account book, but one of likeness to Christ leading to transformation into the likeness of God. The latter is a thought more at home in Eastern forms of Christianity than in Western. It reminds us that humanity was originally made in the image of God, and that the meaning of redemption has to do in part with the restoration of that image. This restoration begins in the present life, as we clothe ourselves with Christ (Gal. 3:27–28) the last Adam (1 Cor. 15:45–49), and thus also with a new self that is renewed in the image of the Creator (Col. 3:10–14). The more we "put on the Lord Jesus Christ" (Rom. 13:14)—the more it is true that "as he is, so are we in this world"—the more confident we can be of our final transformation into the divine likeness at the Judgment. Indeed, because of our likeness to Christ now, there is a sense in which that transformation has already begun; because we love as he loved, we have already "passed from death to life" (3:14). In this sense, part of our confidence about the Last Judgment is that we already live the eternal life that is to be given then, so that the Judgment has, so to speak, already taken place for us (John 5:24).

Thus in perfect love, in the love of God brought to its conclusion in our love for one another, there is no fear. "No fear of the Judgment" is what the author obviously means, given the context. However, if we have no fear of that, what need have we to fear any of the trials and traumas that this life can bring? God's love, brought to its completion in our love, casts out fear, expels it, throws it away. Indeed, fear is a sign or a symptom of not having reached the completed state of love, the love that gives up its life, or at the very least its goods, for others (3:16–17). This love has no use for fear, and pitches it out like trash through an open door. Rather than trying to heighten his readers' fear of the Last Judgment, rather than painting for them a terrifying picture of the fate of "sinners in the hands of an angry God" (as the great preacher Jonathan Edwards titled one of his most famous sermons), our author holds out the prospect of fear done away with. I noted above that 1 John seems to avoid portraying God as a vindictive judge. This is evident not least in the author's rejection of fear as a feature of Christian life and as a tool for urging people to live that life as children of God ought to do.

LOVING GOD
1 John 4:19–5:5

4:19 **We love because he first loved us. 20 Those who say, "I love God," and hate their brothers or sisters, are liars; for those who do not love a brother or sister whom they have seen, cannot love God whom they have not seen. 21 The commandment we have from him is this: those who love God must love their brothers and sisters also.**

5:1 **Everyone who believes that Jesus is the Christ has been born of God, and everyone who loves the parent loves the child. 2 By this we know that we love the children of God, when we love God and obey his commandments. 3 For the love of God is this, that we obey his commandments. And his commandments are not burdensome, 4 for whatever is born of God conquers the world. And this is the victory that conquers the world, our faith. 5 Who is it that conquers the world but the one who believes that Jesus is the Son of God?**

The preceding passage very thoroughly lays out the relationship between God's love for us and our love for one another. Up to this point, however, and perhaps somewhat surprisingly, 1 John has said almost nothing about our love for *God* (the only probable exception being 2:5). Now the author turns to that subject. The transition from love for one another to love for God is made by the somewhat ambiguous verse 19, which speaks of "love" without specifying an object. Only in verse 20 does it become clear that the object is God. There is another ambiguity about verse 19 as well: the verb translated "we love" in most English versions could also be rendered "*Let us* love," and probably should be. Since each of the two preceding sections begins with a call to love (4:7, using exactly the same verb, and 4:11), verse 19 should also be understood as such a call. The only difference is that no object of the love is expressed, in order to make the transition; otherwise, the thought is exactly the same as in 4:11, namely, that we ought to love, since God has loved us.

There is an oddly smooth flow of thought from 4:19 through 5:5, odd because the actual content changes considerably. In 4:19, the subject is love; in 5:5, it is belief in Jesus. Yet it is hard to pinpoint the exact spot at which the subject changes. "Love" flows into "love for God," and love for God is then said to demand love for one's brothers and sisters. The reason for this is that one cannot love a parent without loving the children. If we love God, we must love God's children, that is, God's *other* children, our brothers and sisters. God's children are then defined as those who believe that Jesus is the Christ. If we want to show our love for God's children, we need to show our love for God, and that means obeying God's commandments. Such obedience is not difficult, since God's children conquer the world—conquer it, that is, by their faith, namely, their belief that Jesus is the Son of God. The logical connections at each point are generally clear; the connection between 5:1 and 5:5 is very obvious. Yet the logical connection from the beginning of the passage to its end is not obvious at all. The real connection, though, has to do not with ordinary logic but with the underlying unity between belief and action in the thought of 1 John. The author can, of course, distinguish between believing in Jesus and loving one another, but he makes no real separation between them. This is implied in 3:23, which places both of them under the heading of the commandment of God, and then leads into the discussion of first one and then the other in 4:1–18. But confession of Jesus and love for one another were already intertwined in 4:14–16, and here they simply seem to flow into each other.

This passage, near the end of 1 John, takes us back in many ways to its

first major unit, 1:5–2:11. The expression "Those who say, 'I love God' "
in verse 20 is strongly reminiscent of the "If we say" claims and the claims
to know and abide in God in that earlier passage, and also reminiscent of
the mention of God's love in 2:5. The reference to lying, in relation to
inconsistency between such claims and the actions of the people who make
them; the discussion of loving and hating one's brothers and sisters; and
the reference to God's commandments also remind us of the earlier passage. By harking back to the beginning, the author indicates that he is
drawing his exhortation to a close. He may also be alluding not just to possible human conduct in general but specifically to that of his opponents,
whom he probably also had in mind in 1:5–2:11. It is they who make
claims of close relationship with God, while failing to show loving concern
for their brothers and sisters (3:15–17). The proof offered here for the
charge that they are lying uses a form of logical argument that was common in ancient rhetoric, the argument from the lesser instance (loving visible people) to the greater (loving the invisible God). If you do not love in
a case where your love can be readily verified, the author contends, there
is no way to accept your claim to love in a case that cannot be verified by
human observation. More significantly, 1 John 4:12 already asserted that
God, whom no one has seen, is made known in the believers' love for one
another (see the comments on that verse). How can one claim to love God
then, if one refuses to take part in the very means by which God is
revealed? To claim to love God without loving one's brothers and sisters
is to claim to love a God whom one does not even know (4:8).

At this point, in verse 21, the author goes back to the notion of the *com-*
mandment to love, not seen since 3:23. In discussing that verse, I noted that
there is some possibility that it is related to Jesus' teaching about the two
greatest commandments, to love God and to love one's neighbor (Mark
12:28–34). The resemblance here is even closer, since this passage actually
speaks of loving God. Elsewhere in 1 John, commandments are always
thought of as coming from God rather than from Jesus, and the context
here also suggests that "from him" means "from God." Of course, this
teaching of Jesus was about commandments in the Torah, the Law of
Moses, and those commandments are also naturally understood to have
been given by God. There is thus a good chance that, without citing Jesus
specifically, our author is here presenting an idea that derives ultimately
from his teaching: that the essence of God's will is that we love God and
love one another.

In what follows, however, the thought patterns are the ones typical of
the Gospel and letters of John (although as usual the writer of the letters

does not express himself as clearly as the Gospel). This thought pattern begins with the premise that to love God means obeying God's commandments. These commandments are to believe in Jesus and to love one another (1 John 3:23). (We should note that in the Gospel of John, it is those who love *Jesus* who keep his commandment to love one another: John 13:34; 14:15, 21–24; 15:10, 12, 17.) In fact, since those who believe are born of God (John 1:12–13), and since those who love the parent will naturally also love the child, obeying the commandment to believe and so becoming a child of God already implies loving those others who believe and so are also God's children. Here again we see how inseparable belief and mutual love are for this author. In his way of understanding the Christian life as a loving response to the loving initiative taken by God, the response of belief necessarily entails the response of love for other believers. To believe is to be a child of God; and what child does not love his or her parents' other children? (It is assumed, of course, that the family of God is not dysfunctional! Or perhaps we should say, it is assumed that those who truly are and desire to remain part of this family will do all in their power to keep it from becoming dysfunctional.)

First John 5:1 is the first and only time that our author associates birth from God with right belief in Jesus rather than with right actions, meaning specifically love (contrast 2:29; 3:9–10; 4:7; 5:18). This association, which is typical of the Fourth Gospel (John 1:12–13, just noted), seems intended to reintroduce the subject of belief in Jesus, last seen in 4:1–6. Belief then becomes the topic of discussion throughout the rest of the book, just as love has been the primary topic since 4:7. It is also worth noting that one of the parallel belief formulas in 5:1 and 5:5 speaks of Jesus as the Christ (Messiah), and the other speaks of him as the Son of God. Taken together, these two terms form the complete statement of belief in "his Son Jesus Christ" that is the object of the commandment in 3:23, and also the aim of the Gospel of John (20:31). (Note also the use of the phrase "his Son Jesus Christ" in 1 John 5:20 and the confessional formulas in 2:22–23; 4:2–3, 15.) It is not only the theme of belief but this particular formulation of it that dominates 1 John from here on. Indeed, I will note several further allusions to John 20:31 later in chapter 5.

One reason that John 20:31, like the Gospel of John as a whole, insists so strongly on belief in Jesus as Messiah and Son of God is that the Christian community for which that Gospel was written was suffering considerable persecution for their public confession of precisely this belief. By the time 1 John was written, circumstances had changed. The community was no longer a group of people primarily of Jewish birth that was facing pressure from outside itself, namely, from the synagogue authorities. Rather, the difficulties were now coming from within, from stresses and schisms brought on (at least in our author's view) by a group that "went out from us" (2:19; see the Introduction to 1 John). The claim that those who believe in Jesus as Messiah and Son of God are born of God was originally a defensive claim, used to sustain a Christian group that was running the risk of expulsion from the synagogue community, and therefore of being cut off from their self-understanding as people of God. In 1 John, this claim is becoming more of an offensive weapon, a means of defining who is in and who is out of the Christian circle. If those who make this confession of faith are children of God, and therefore are to be loved, does that mean that those who do not make it (namely, the author's opponents) are not God's children, and so are excluded from the company of "brothers and sisters" who should be loved? The author does not say this and does not quite seem to have this question on his agenda; but it would certainly be possible to read 2 John and draw just such a conclusion. By proposing a traditional formula as a test of true belief, 1 John opens the door to the use of creedal and dogmatic tests to determine who is an authentic member of the church and who deserves to be excommunicated and placed under an anathema.

Depending on the Christian tradition to which you belong, you may find this a necessary and healthy development or a dangerous one; but it does not seem to have done much to promote the spirit of love that 1 John works so hard to cultivate. Yet if our author really sees belief and love as inseparable responses to the love of God in Jesus Christ, then we must allow him to stress the former equally with the latter. If it is impossible, in his thinking, to believe in Jesus Christ in any true sense without also loving one's brothers and sisters just as Jesus did, then it is also impossible to love one another with the love that comes from God unless one acknowledges the revelation of that love as God chose to make it, namely, in the human reality of Jesus. Divine love has been made known in the human death of Jesus. To downplay the significance of that death, that reality, as the opponents apparently were doing, leaves one cut off from the access to divine love that God has made available. To accept the revelation of God as love in Jesus Christ means loving one's brothers and sisters; to love one's brothers and sisters means to love the God whose children they are, and that means accepting the divine self-revelation on God's terms. It is all one love, all one response to God's love, as far as 1 John is concerned. The door may be opened to a kind of formal dogmatism that simply demands agreement to a formula without considering what is in a person's heart or life; but our author is very far from going through that door himself. For him, belief that Jesus is the Christ, the Son of God, is not a formality but a living, freely chosen consent to the love of God, which cannot happen apart from the offering of one's life in love for one's brothers and sisters—any more than that self-offering can take place apart from genuine confession of the human Jesus as the one in whom God's own self-giving love has been revealed.

First John 5:2 both expresses the unity of belief and love, and makes the transition from the discussion of love to that of belief. In the process, the author says something that is surprising and rather difficult to understand: "By this we know that we love the children of God, when we love God and obey his commandments." Shouldn't it say just the reverse, that we know we love God when we love God's children, as indeed the author has just gotten through saying? How does loving God show that we love God's children? Can the flow of the logic really be reversed so easily? Apparently, the answer must be yes. If "everyone who loves the parent loves the child," then everyone who loves the child must also love the parent, that is, those who love God's children must also love God; and loving God could not be compatible with rejecting God's commandments. (The same point is made with even less clarity in 2 John 6.) What is really happening here, however, is a shift in the reference of "commandment." The most recently discussed commandment was that of love for brothers and sisters (4:21). But we cannot simply plug that commandment alone into 5:2 without producing a meaningless circular argument: we know that we love God's children when we love God's children. Thus the "commandments" in 5:2 must also include the other commandment listed in 3:23, that of belief in Jesus, a subject that has just been reintroduced in 5:1. Yet belief does not completely take over the meaning of "commandments" in these verses, since in that case verses 3–5 would also become circular: it is not hard to believe in Jesus, because we believe in Jesus. Thus the "commandments" in 5:2–3 include both the commandment to love one another and the commandment to believe in Jesus. But the emphasis is shifting (so subtly that it is a bit hard to follow) to the latter, as the author makes his transition to what will then be the subject of the following passages.

The language of commandment in relation to love and belief raises certain questions, some of which I addressed in the comments on 3:23. Here, the author considers the possibility that such commandments might be more than we can handle. No, he says, they are not too much for us, because as children of God we have conquered the world. This conquest has been mentioned before, in 2:13–14, in terms of conquering the evil one (who holds power over the world, according to 5:19), and in 4:4–5, in terms of conquering the opponents (who are "from the world"). As always, the writer's aim is to encourage the readers and not discourage them, and so here again he reminds them of the confidence that they can have as they seek to live as loving and obedient children of God. The world, the system of human society that rejects and opposes God and God's commandments, will naturally try to keep them from carrying out their loving obedience. The world, in this sense, is not only hostile to God's children (3:1, 13), but is understood as seeking to prevent them from obeying God's commandments, because it is focused instead on self-gratification and self-will (see 2:15–17, and the comments there). The readers need not fear this opposition, however. Precisely as children of God, they have conquered the world; they are able to resist sin, and the evil one cannot touch them (5:18). This is because the faith that makes them children of God is their belief that Jesus is the Christ, the Son of God (5:1, 5), and it was Jesus, the Son of God, who made the original conquest of the world (John 16:33). "Whatever is born of God conquers the world," and this means not only God's Son Jesus, but all God's children who believe in him.

TESTIMONY TO JESUS
1 John 5:6–12

5:6 **This is the one who came by water and blood, Jesus Christ, not with the water only but with the water and the blood. And the Spirit is the one that testifies, for the Spirit is the truth. ⁷ There are three that testify: ⁸ the Spirit and the water and the blood, and these three agree. ⁹ If we receive human testimony, the testimony of God is greater; for this is the testimony of God that he has testified to his Son. ¹⁰ Those who believe in the Son of God have the testimony in their hearts. Those who do not believe in God have made him a liar by not believing in the testimony that God has given concerning his Son. ¹¹ And this is the testimony: God gave us eternal life, and this life is in his Son. ¹² Whoever has the Son has life; whoever does not have the Son of God does not have life.**

Now that the subject of belief in Jesus has been reintroduced in the preceding passage, it becomes the primary focus of attention, although here it is discussed in terms of "testimony." Just as the preceding passage harked back to a section of the text near the beginning of 1 John (1:5–2:11), so this passage is reminiscent of the book's prologue (1:1–4), in that both speak of testimony to Jesus and of eternal life. First John 5:6–12 divides fairly easily into two smaller units, 5:6–8 and 5:9–12. In the first of these, the title "Christ" ("Messiah") is used and the testimony to him is given by the Spirit, the water, and the blood. In the second, we find the title "Son of God," and the testimony is given by God. The separation of the two titles follows 5:1 and 5; but, as in those verses, the effect is actually to unify the entire passage, since the two are really part of one single title, God's "Son Jesus Christ" (3:23; 5:20). The author is signalling that his book is drawing near its end, both by the references back to its beginning, and by alluding to a climactic passage near the end of the Gospel of John (20:31), which also calls for faith that Jesus is "the Messiah, the Son of God," a faith that brings "life in his name." Indeed, that verse was probably the original ending of the Fourth Gospel; following it, chapter 21 appears to be an appendix. The frequent allusions to John 20:31 in the final chapter of 1 John suggest that the author is deliberately echoing the ending of the Gospel at the end of his own composition.

Despite this structural clarity, there are aspects of this passage that make it difficult to understand and interpret. Some have to do with what the author is saying, and some with how he says it. One matter, however, has to do with what words he really wrote, and we should deal with this first.

If you look up this passage in the King James Version, you will find that verses 7 and 8 are considerably longer there than they are in the NRSV text given above, and in most other modern translations. In the King James, they read as follows: "⁷For there are three that bear record in heaven, the Father, the Word, and the Holy Ghost: and these three are one. ⁸And there are three that bear witness in earth, the Spirit, and the water, and the blood: and these three agree in one." The extra words are "in heaven, the Father, the Word, and the Holy Ghost: and these three are one. And there are three that bear witness in earth." The reason for this has to do not with the meaning of the words in the text but with what words are actually there. The nature of the problem and how it arose is a bit of a long story, but it is worth at least summarizing in order to show how this difference among Bible translations came about.

First John, like the other New Testament writings, was written in Greek; and as with all books in the ancient world, copies of the original manuscript had to be produced by hand in order for others to read it besides those to whom it was originally addressed. Copies were made from those copies, and so on down through the years, with the result that though the original and many of the early copies have been lost we do have a fairly large number of Greek manuscripts of 1 John (generally grouped together with 2 and 3 John, and some of the other shorter letters of the New Testament). Of course, as Christianity spread to areas where people did not speak Greek, the biblical texts were translated into other languages (such as Latin, the Coptic dialects of Egypt, and so on), and copies were made of those translations. In the process of all this copying, it is natural that mistakes were made, so that it is rare for any two handwritten copies of the same New Testament book to be perfectly identical. Obviously, what we would like to know is the wording of the original manuscript, as it left its author's hand. The scholarly discipline that tries to reach this goal is called *textual criticism*. First John 5:7–8 presents a well-known text critical problem that has some unusual features.

Most of the Greek manuscripts of 1 John have only the words that are present in the NRSV and other modern translations; only a very few include the extra words that are translated in the King James Version, and those few are all quite late in date. In the Latin translation known as the Vulgate, however, there are many manuscripts with those words. Textual critics have determined that the words were probably added into the Latin translation, perhaps in the fourth century, in order to deal with certain theological disputes of that time. Eventually, they were translated from Latin back into Greek and added into a small number of Greek manuscripts. Unfortunately, when printing presses began to be used in Europe, one of these manuscripts was used to produce some of the early printed editions of the Greek New Testament. These early editions, in turn, formed the basis of the commonly printed text of the Greek New Testament in Europe during the Reformation period, and indeed down until modern times. It was from this text that the New Testament of the King James Version was translated, and in this way the extra words in 1 John 5:7–8 came to be included in the classic English translation. As powerful and influential as that translation has been, we must respectfully conclude that this is a case in which it can no longer be used, because it is based on a text that is now known to be incorrect. The text critical study of the last 150 years has shown conclusively that the original Greek text of 1 John 5:7–8 contained only the words that are translated in most modern English versions, including the NRSV.

The question remains, however, what do those original words mean? Why is it significant that Jesus Christ came "not with the water only but with the water and the blood"? Why did the author think it so important to deny that he came "with the water only," and how did he come "with the water and the blood"? How is it that the Spirit testifies, and for that matter how do the water and the blood testify? We may hope that the readers to whom 1 John was originally addressed understood these things more or less readily. For us, however, a bit of digging is required.

Verse 6 has some features that suggest the author is (a) arguing against someone else and (b) presenting a formula for the confession of faith. The words "not with the water only" imply that somebody else must have said that Jesus Christ *did* come "with the water," and only with the water. That would presumably be the opponents against whom the author has been arguing elsewhere in 1 John. The same argumentative tone and concern for exact definition appear in 4:1–3, which is also another of the few places where 1 John speaks of Jesus Christ's "coming" (see the comments on that passage; the other is 5:21). The similarity in wording and interests suggests that, just as 4:2 is a model formula for confession of Jesus, so also is "came by water and blood." The author, then, seems to be proposing a kind of standard for the confession of belief that Jesus is the Christ and the Son of God, the faith that makes one a child of God and allows one to conquer "the world," according to 5:1–5. To confess that faith rightly, one must confess that this Jesus Christ "came by water and blood."

What could this "coming by water and blood" mean, then? The most closely similar expression elsewhere in the New Testament is found in John 19:34–35, which tells how the piercing of Jesus' side at his death produced a flow of blood and water, and emphasizes the truthfulness of the testimony to this event. Since not only testimony but the Spirit is prominent in our passage, we should also bear in mind John 1:32–34, where John the Baptist testifies that he saw the Spirit descend on Jesus, which was a sign given to him by the One who sent him to baptize with water. Indeed, testimony to Jesus is a very prominent theme throughout the Gospel of John (see, for example, John 5:31–47; 8:17–18; 15:26–27). Thus another factor in understanding what this passage is about is the likelihood that the author, the readers, and probably also the opponents were thinking about texts from the Gospel of John, or at least elements in the tradition familiar to them, a tradition that we know from this Gospel.

Given all this, what do we make of the contrast between "water and blood" and "water only"? Where water alone appears (John 1:32–34), it has to do with baptism, which is natural in a Christian context. Specifically, it has to do with *Jesus'* baptism, the occasion when the Spirit descended from heaven to rest on him. The idea that he came "with water only," against which 1 John is arguing, may then have something to do with Jesus' baptism. For instance, the opponents may have claimed (as some second-century groups are known to have done) that what happened at Jesus' baptism was that the divine Christ, a spirit from heaven, descended on the human Jesus. For them, this was the significant moment or at least the significant beginning point for the divine revelation in Jesus Christ. Later events—including the death of Jesus—would have had little or no significance for revelation or salvation, in their thinking. (It is even possible, though this is pure speculation, that the opponents saw in John 19:30, where Jesus "gives up the spirit," an indication that the heavenly spirit left Jesus at his death, which therefore meant his death had no "spiritual" meaning.) Not so our author, for whom the "coming" of Jesus Christ, that is, his coming to bring salvation, did not occur in water only, but in "the water *and the blood.*" The mention of blood would lead us to think of the death of Jesus, even without the combination of blood and water in John 19:34–35. For 1 John, then, it is not the descent of the heavenly spirit on the human Jesus at his baptism, but the death of Jesus Christ that is the true moment of revelation and salvation. Our author has emphasized the saving significance of Jesus' death a number of times (1:7; 2:2; 4:9–10), and this significance is no doubt also part of the reason why he insists on the confession of "Jesus Christ as having come in flesh" in 4:2. Of course, it also goes along with his claim that it was in Jesus' sacrifice of his own life that the love of God was made known, so that those who believe in him are bound to give up their own interests out of love for others as well.

The opponents apparently wanted a tidy, clean, purely spiritual event, such as the baptism of Jesus, to be the means of divine revelation and the coming of salvation. It may have been inconceivable to them that spiritual salvation could come through material means; presumably, they shared the widespread conviction that spirit and mind were superior, and indeed opposed, to body and matter. First John insists that salvation did come through Jesus' death—his bloody and violent death, the death of a man suffering oppression at the hands of the world's greatest political power. Nothing could be more physical, more caught up in the material world with its bodily pains and its social shame and its political tyrannies, than a crucifixion. When Paul speaks of the cross as a "stumbling block" and "foolishness" (1 Cor. 1:18–2:5), this is what he has in mind. We are used to thinking of the cross as a religious symbol, but that was not its meaning when Christianity began. If it symbolized anything, it symbolized shame and defeat, the weakness of occupied territories and enslaved persons, and the brutal power of the imperial government to enforce the social and political status quo. It may be the greatest miracle in early Christianity that when Christian apostles and preachers declared that a man who had suffered this fate was the Savior sent from God, anybody believed it at all. It is likewise not surprising that some groups, especially those who were concerned to make the Christian message more palatable and understandable to their contemporaries (see comments on 4:1–6), might want to restrict the revelation in Christ to "the water only."

Granted that this is at least close to what the author was trying to argue, where does the testimony of the Spirit fit in? The opponents clearly claimed the Spirit as the source of their teaching; that is the point of the author's exhortation to "test the spirits" in 4:1–3. The author seems to make the same claim for his own teaching in his references to the "anointing" that teaches the readers all they need to know, including that they should abide in Jesus as they had known him from the beginning (2:20–27). This anointing is said to be "true," just as the Spirit is "the Spirit of truth" (4:6), an expression familiar from the Gospel of John (14:17; 16:13; note also 4:23–24). Indeed, according to John 15:26, the Spirit of truth testifies to Jesus. All this helps us to understand the background of the statement in 1 John 5:6 that "the Spirit is the one that testifies, for the Spirit is the truth." In this verse, the author seems to be appealing to the Holy Spirit, the Spirit of truth, as the one who testifies that Jesus Christ "came by water and blood." This also can be understood against the background of the Gospel of John, for, as noted earlier, in John 19:34–35, not only does blood and water flow from Jesus' side when it is pierced after his death, but we read that "he who saw this has testified so that you also may believe. His testimony is true, and he knows that he tells the truth." If the testimony is true, then its ultimate source and confirmation must be the Spirit of truth who testifies to Jesus. (Note that immediately following the promise in John 15:26, Jesus' disciples are also called on to testify. John 14:26 and 16:12–15 suggest that this Christian community saw all teaching about Jesus as the work of the Spirit of truth.)

Thus it seems likely that the author of 1 John is claiming that it is the Spirit of truth, the giver of all true testimony, who testifies in John 19:34–35 (or the tradition behind it) to the coming of Jesus Christ by water and blood. Contrary to the claims of the opponents, the Spirit does not confirm their teaching about the spiritual Christ, but affirms the incarnation, the coming of Jesus Christ in the flesh, and the saving significance of his death. For 1 John, the Spirit is present not only in new, creative developments, but also in the tradition that has been handed down, which embodies the Spirit's previous testimony. New teaching that fundamentally contradicts this tradition, such as that of the opponents, with their denial that salvation in the divine Christ and Son of God is present in the human Jesus, cannot really be from the Spirit. Of course, the opponents appealed to other elements within the same tradition, those that stressed the divine glory of Christ rather than his physical, human qualities. The real problem was how to decide which part of the tradition should be considered central, so central that it would determine what new developments and interpretations could be regarded as legitimate. For 1 John, this central part was the claim that the eternal, invisible God was revealed in a visible, mortal human being—indeed, was revealed precisely in his mortality, his brutal death on a Roman cross. This is a difficult, paradoxical assertion, but 1 John is right to maintain that it is the essential claim of the Gospel of John. For our author, the key that makes this claim intelligible is love. God chose to be revealed in this way because God is love and nothing could better reveal divine love than such an act of utter self-sacrifice. This is what the Spirit attests when it testifies to the water and the blood, and so enables them to "testify" also. These three witnesses (compare Deut. 19:15) "agree," or more literally translated, they "are at one" or "attest to the one thing," or (as the New Jerusalem Bible renders it) they "coincide." All of them point to the reality and the meaning of Jesus' humanity, including his death in self-giving love.

From the testimony of the Spirit, the water, and the blood, the author turns to the testimony of God. This is contrasted with human testimony, which may perhaps mean specifically the testimony of John the Baptist, which is also contrasted with God's testimony in John 5:31–38. There Jesus actually says he does *not* receive the Baptist's testimony, so our author may be getting in a subtle dig at the opponents, if they relied heavily on that testimony in their claim that the Christ came only by water. At any rate, it is of course the testimony of God that is of ultimate value. Verse 9 introduces this concept, and seems about to specify what God's testimony is when verse 10 intervenes as a kind of parenthesis. By repeating the same words at the end of verse 10 as at the end of verse 9, the author finds his place again, and finally gives the content of God's testimony in verse 11. If the parenthesis in verse 10 is not enough to lead the reader astray, the author also throws in one of those little grammatical ambiguities that can make 1 John so difficult for translators and interpreters (see the comments on 3:19–20). In the NRSV rendering of the second half of verse 9 ("for this is the testimony of God that he has testified to his Son"), the words "for" and "that" translate two occurrences of the same word. This may be a plausible translation, but it leaves one thing very unclear: what does "this" refer to? In other words, what *is* the testimony? It would probably be better to translate the Greek word with "for" in both cases: "*for* this is the testimony of God—*for* he has testified to his Son." The author simply affirms that God has testified, and goes on to warn against rejecting this testimony (v. 10), while leaving the content of the testimony unspecified until verse 11.

The point of the parenthesis in verse 10 is simply that since God has testified it would be foolhardy to spurn this testimony by refusing to believe in the Son of God. Because God has testified to the Son, to believe in the Son is to believe in God; the same is true of disbelieving. (The logic and the language here are reminiscent of John 3:18, 33, 36, another passage that involves John the Baptist.) Moreover, those who do believe have God's testimony "in themselves" (despite the NRSV, the Greek does not speak of "hearts"). We should be careful not to drift off into speculation about an "inner witness" of the Spirit here. The testimony of God that believers have in themselves is named quite precisely in verse 11: it is the gift of eternal life itself, a gift given in the Son of God, that is, in Jesus. Those who "have the Son," who "believe in the Son of God"—that is, those who confess the identity of the human Jesus as the divine Son of God (compare 2:22–24)—are the ones who have this eternal life in themselves. The very presence of eternal life in those who confess Jesus as Son of God, who "confess Jesus Christ as having come in flesh" (4:2), is the testimony of God that this confession is true.

Eternal life means not only life that never ends but "the life of eternity." It refers not just to the quantity of life, but to its *quality*. It means a life that is *characterized* by eternity, by the world of God that transcends the present world. Eternal life is divine life, the very life of God. The ultimate testimony to the truth of the incarnation is eternal life, because "this life is in his Son" (compare 1 John 1:2). The whole point of the Gospel of John is that eternal life was offered to the human race in Jesus Christ and was received by those who believed in him (see, for example, John 3:16, 36; 11:25). Indeed, divine life as such, the life of God, is present in Jesus, the Word made flesh (John 1:3–4; 5:26; 14:6–7), and those who believe in him have this divine life now, without waiting for the Last Judgment (John 5:24; 11:26). We can also sense the thought of John 20:31 once again in the background of what is said here. Belief that Jesus is the Son of God brings eternal life: this is the doctrine that is absolutely fundamental to the Christian tradition and the Christian community that produced both the Gospel and the letters of John. Here near the end of his writing, our author insists once more that this doctrine undermines the opponents' theology of salvation through a spiritual Christ unconnected, or at least unconcerned, with material flesh. If divine life itself is in Jesus the Son of God and is available in him to those who believe, then denying that the human Jesus is the Son means rejecting the very testimony that God has given about him.

WE KNOW THAT WE BELONG TO GOD
1 John 5:13–21

5:13 **I write these things to you who believe in the name of the Son of God, so that you may know that you have eternal life.**

[14] **And this is the boldness we have in him, that if we ask anything according to his will, he hears us.** [15] **And if we know that he hears us in whatever we ask, we know that we have obtained the requests made of him.** [16] **If you see your brother or sister committing what is not a mortal sin, you will ask, and God will give life to such a one—to those whose sin is not mortal. There is sin that is mortal; I do not say that you should pray about that.** [17] **All wrongdoing is sin, but there is sin that is not mortal.**

[18] **We know that those who are born of God do not sin, but the one who was born of God protects them, and the evil one does not touch them.** [19] **We know that we are God's children, and that the whole world lies under the power of the evil one.** [20] **And we know that the Son of God has come and has given us understanding so that we may know him who is true; and we are in him who is true, in his Son Jesus Christ. He is the true God and eternal life.**

[21] **Little children, keep yourselves from idols.**

The original conclusion of the Gospel of John was probably at the end of chapter 20; chapter 21 seems to be an appendix added at a slightly later time. Since 1 John 5:13 bears such a close resemblance to John 20:31 and since the material that follows in 5:14–21 is so rambling and miscellaneous, it is tempting to see an original ending and a later appendix here as well. Indeed, 5:13 gives a very good statement of the basic purpose of 1 John. Yet since the author has repeatedly echoed John 20:31 throughout this final chapter, verse 13 can also be seen as simply summing up what has gone immediately before it. Moreover, this verse is itself echoed in verse 20, with its references to the Son of God and eternal life, so that there is at least that much coherence to 5:13–21 as a whole. Indeed, those same references also echo the opening verses of 1 John, thereby tying the entire composition together. Verse 13, then, may be seen not as a conclusion but as a transition, belonging both to what comes before it and to what comes after it and so connecting the two.

Within this final passage, there is, as I mentioned, not nearly as much evidence of careful structuring as we have seen in some other parts of 1 John. Various themes that have been significant throughout the book are touched on (prayer, sin, the children of God, the world and the evil one, God, the Son, eternal life), but surprisingly, the main themes—love for one another and right belief in Jesus—are not very obviously present.

Some connections from one part to another can be noticed: verses 14 and 15 are concerned with prayer, which is mentioned again in verses 16–17, whose subject is sin; sin is then taken up again in verse 18, which also speaks of "the evil one," and that reference leads into verse 19. One theme that does occur throughout verses 13–21, helping to give them some unity, is that of knowledge. The author wants the readers to know that they have eternal life (v. 13); they also know that God hears their prayers (v. 15). In particular, the last unit, verses 18–21, speaks of three things that the believing community knows: that God's children do not sin, that they themselves belong to God, and that the Son of God has enabled them to know God. As we will see, all three of these have to do with the contrast between God's children and the forces of evil. Indeed, the things that are known in verses 13 and 15 can also be seen as aspects of the life of the children of God.

First John contains plenty of evidence that the author's purpose in writing was to encourage the readers, to bolster their confidence in their relationship with God—assuming that they, unlike his opponents, share the author's faith in the human Jesus as the divine Son of God. (In the Greek, "who believe in the name of the Son of God" is in an emphatic position at the end of verse 13; this echoes both John 20:31 and John 1:12.) The author has also already made several references to his purposes (1:4; 2:1) and reasons (2:12–14) for writing. Moreover, he has assured his readers that he is writing not because of any ignorance on their part but because of their knowledge (2:21). Given all that, 5:13 probably does not mean that he thinks he must tell them they have eternal life because they don't already know it. Rather, his purpose for writing includes the desire to reinforce what they already know and build up their confidence, perhaps in the face of uncertainties caused by the teaching and the departure of the opponents.

As part of this reinforcement, the author reminds the readers of the confidence they have when praying (vv. 14–15). This certainty of being heard is something that "we know." The same subject was discussed in similar terms in 3:21–23. The sequence of events in prayer is presented in a simple, indeed almost simplistic, manner: we ask according to God's will, God hears us, and we obtain our requests. The key phrase is "according to God's will." This could mean simply that we get what we request if the request is what God wills, but it may also have a deeper sense. God's will here may mean something similar to God's commandments in 3:21–23. In the comments on those verses, I have explored the significance of the relationship with God that results in observing God's commandments in the life of prayer, so I need not repeat those reflections here.

Now the author moves from the answering of prayers in general to the specific prayer that should be made for one's brother or sister who has sinned. This is a kind of prayer that may be unfamiliar to many of us today. Our responses to sin within the church may range from indifference to silent anguish to silent anger to not-so-silent gossip. We may think it is none of our business or we may not be sure whom we should tell about it. First John assumes that sin is our business, if the church is a community of brothers and sisters in an intimate relationship of love for one another. But the only one whom the author suggests we tell is God. The sin in question need not have been committed against the one who is doing the praying, nor does 1 John speak of confronting the sinner, whether in public or in private (contrast Matt. 18:15–17). It is a matter of one Christian observing another Christian's improper conduct and taking it to God. There is a certain humility in this, since the one praying makes no assumption of moral superiority—the author does not recommend asking that the sinner learn to be righteous like the person doing the praying. Certainly there is no thought of one person having the authority to admonish the other or of taking the matter up with a third party, resulting in the disgrace of the sinner. It remains between the praying Christian and God. There is not even any mention of confession, as there is in 1 John 1:5–2:2, where it is Jesus who intercedes with God for sinners (see comments there; compare also James 5:14–20 and note John 20:23). The biblical models for this kind of intercessory prayer include Abraham (Gen. 18:23–33; 20:7) and Moses (Exod. 32:9–14). The result is life for the sinner, presumably meaning the restoration of eternal life, which he or she, as a brother or sister in the believing community, would already have possessed. There is some ambiguity about who "gives life" to the sinner. The NRSV rendering of this verse is rather free. Somewhat more literally, it might run, "If someone sees his/her brother committing a sin that is not mortal, he/she will pray and he/she will give life." Most likely the giver of life is God, not the person praying, but that is not quite certain.

There are other ambiguities in verses 16–17 as well. In particular what is "sin that is mortal" or "a sin that leads to death," as the *New International Version* puts it? It is natural to be curious about this, although we should avoid the kind of morbid curiosity that makes us either afraid we have committed this sin or hopeful that someone else has. A couple of things can be eliminated at once. The language here is entirely different from the saying in Mark 3:28–30 about the blasphemy against the Holy Spirit that cannot be forgiven, and there is no reason to connect the two. There is also no suggestion here that sins can be ranked, from the minor ones that can be overlooked up to the really bad ones: "all wrongdoing is sin" (v. 17). Yet there is sin that leads to death, and the author seems to assume that the readers know what it is; at any rate, he gives very little indication of what he means. In the Hebrew Bible, the worship of other gods or a deliberate rejection of God is sometimes spoken of as beyond atonement or prayer (for example, Num. 15:27–31; 1 Sam. 2:22–25; Isa. 22:12–14; Jer. 7:16–20; 14:7–12). Within the New Testament, we may note Hebrews 6:4–8 and 10:26–30, which also concern deliberate rejection of Christianity after one has once embraced it. The Gospel of John, perhaps most significantly of all, speaks of Jesus' opponents as "dying in their sins" (something obviously similar to "a sin that leads to death") because of their rejection of him (John 8:21–24). Finally, we may get some help from considering what 1 John itself has to say about life and death. Eternal life comes from believing in Jesus, that is, from believing that the human Jesus is the divine Christ, the Son of God, who revealed divine love by giving up his life in order that we might live (1 John 4:9–10; 5:11–13). Thus, to reject this belief is to lose eternal life; it is a rejection that leads to death. It is also tantamount to rejecting God, who sent Jesus and has testified to him (5:9–11). On the other hand, 1 John also says that we pass from death to life when we love one another, laying down our lives for one another as Jesus did for us (3:14–17). Refusal to love, refusal to show active, material care for our brothers and sisters, would then also lead to death, since it would keep us from eternal life. What 1 John means by the "sin that leads to death," then, is probably rejection of the human Jesus as God's Son or failure to love one's brothers and sisters, or a combination of the two. Both of these lead away from eternal life and thus toward death; and both of them amount to a rejection of God, who sent and testified to Jesus, and who is love. Belief in Jesus and love for one another, of course, are the primary themes of 1 John. This also means that the fatal sin is what the author's opponents are doing, and no doubt there is a warning here against going over to their side.

We might expect that such a sin would be the very one for which the need for prayer is strongest. Yet 1 John says, "I do not say that you should pray about that." This is not quite a prohibition of praying for the opponents or for others who sin similarly, but it is certainly not an encouragement to do so. The sharpness of the dispute, or the severity of the problems caused by the opponents leaving the community (2:19), or the possibility that the opponents themselves showed no care for their brothers and sisters (3:15, 17; 4:20) may in some sense explain the author's attitude. Yet it is hard to see how these things would justify a refusal to pray for them. If the interpretation of these verses suggested here is at least approximately correct, we may see in them a striking example of the way in which "love for one another" within a limited circle can fall short of Jesus' exhortation to "love your enemies, do good to those who hate you, bless those who curse you, pray for those who abuse you" (Luke 6:27–28).

Apart from the special, drastic case of the sin that leads to death, "all wrongdoing is sin," and Christians should pray for other Christians who sin. At just this point, however, the author creates the most perplexing contradiction in his little book, for he immediately goes on to say that "those who are born of God do not sin"! Previously such inconsistent statements have been separated from one another (1:5–2:2 and 2:28–3:10, respectively). Here, with verses 16–17 comparable to 1:5–2:2 and verse 18a almost exactly repeating 3:9a, they are placed side by side. It is certainly convenient to have the author's thinking regarding sin summarized so neatly, but we are left to wonder what exactly that thinking is! The writer of 1 John appears careless at times, but it seems impossible that any author could fail to recognize a contradiction so blatant or expect readers not to notice it or to overlook it. What do we make of it? Can Christians sin (and be prayed for and forgiven) or can't they?

Some interpreters have sought to solve the problem by suggesting that verses 16–17 refer to one kind of sin and verse 18 to another, specifically, that verse 18 says that those born of God cannot commit the "sin that leads to death." That would be helpful, and certainly the author might say that the opponents, who commit that sin by failing to confess the human Jesus as the Christ and failing to love their brothers and sisters, would not qualify as people "born of God" (compare 4:7; 5:1). Yet there is not the slightest indication that that is what verse 18 really means. After drawing the careful distinction between sin that does and does not lead to death in the preceding verses, it hardly seems likely that the author would simply say "sin" in verse 18 without specifying "the sin that leads to death," if that were what he meant.

A distinction in types of sin does not seem to be the solution, but there is no other readily available solution either. Apparently, the author was simply content with this level of inconsistency, perhaps seeing it as part of the tradition of thought and speech that gave shape to the Gospel of John, where we read that "the Word was with God, and the Word was God" (John 1:1), that "the Father and I are one" (10:30), but also that "the Father is greater than I" (14:28). Paradox and irony are the main methods of communication in the Fourth Gospel, and it would not be surprising to find them appearing in a work so closely related to it as 1 John. Yet the

Gospel's paradoxes seem designed to lead us toward a greater and deeper truth, one that cannot really be expressed in a simple, straightforward statement. It is hard to get that sense at this point in 1 John. If anything, perhaps the paradox here is simply that of Christian life itself. We are given the power to live without sin in our new birth as children of God, and 1 John, like other writers in the New Testament and later, urges us to exercise that power (compare Rom. 6:1–23; 8:1–16). We may and should confidently rely on the "one who was born of God" (v. 18; a title for Jesus found nowhere else in the New Testament, including the Gospel and letters of John) for protection from the evil one. Yet inevitably "the desire of the flesh" (2:16) reasserts itself, and we do sin. Even so, however, all is not lost, for there are the prayers of our brothers and sisters and the atoning sacrifice of Jesus our advocate and the faithfulness and justice of the God who is love (5:16–17; 2:1–2; 1:9). As noted above, the overriding aim of 1 John is encouragement, and (though perhaps defeating his own purpose by his inconsistency) the author here seeks to offer the dual encouragement of empowerment not to sin and restoration when we do sin. It is not an easy gap to bridge, but then, it is not an easy life to live.

Verse 18 is the first of three assurances of the contrast between the children of God and "the evil one," and of their protection from him. The element of assurance is strengthened by the claim that these are things that "we know." The evil one, of course, represents a source of danger, and it is precisely in the midst of such danger that this assurance of protection has meaning. Our author, like most other New Testament writers, has a lively sense of an opposition to God's will that is more than merely human waywardness (2 Cor. 4:4; Eph. 2:2; Rev. 12:9). For the Gospel of John also, the world's rejection of Christ and oppression of his followers is explained by the assertion that it is the devil who rules the world (John 12:31; 14:30; 16:11; 17:15). The Gospel and letters of John do not give any explanation of how this situation came to be; they seem uninterested in tales of cosmic rebellion. The Gospel insists that the world was made by God, through the Word of God, and so owes its existence to the Word (John 1:3, 10), and that God loves the world and desires to save it (John 3:16–17; 12:46–47; 1 John 2:2; 4:9–10, 14). Yet the world as these writers found it seemed so endlessly hostile to God's efforts to save it—hostile to God's love and to God's commandment to love one another and to the divine revelation in the human Jesus—that they could only think, as our author puts it in verse 19, that "the whole world lies under the power of the evil one," however that may have come about.

This is a very grim viewpoint indeed. Many Christians today may even find it a little bit paranoid. Others, however, in less comfortable surroundings, may think that it sounds just about right. Certainly this worldview is more appropriate to a small sect that finds itself under frequent harassment, despite its conviction that it has received life and light from the Creator of the universe, than it is to a "world religion" that has at times in its history been the official religion of some of the world's mightiest powers.

As Christians, especially in the Western world, look around themselves just now, they may sense that they are at a kind of decision point between these two ways of understanding how the believing community relates to the world at large. Are we to try to return to the glory days of the past, seize the levers of control again and assert the supremacy of Christianity over non-Christian ideologies and theologies? Or does the pluralism of today's world offer the possibility of return to a still earlier situation when Christianity was anything but the "established religion" and a cross was not a piece of jewelry? Will the future find us a "moral majority" or a steadfast minority? Those times in its history when Christianity has been most true to its crucified yet risen Lord and has been at its most creative, theologically, morally, and spiritually, have often been the times when it was a minority, or when a minority within Christianity sought to restore it to a greater faithfulness. Yet with that kind of status often comes the sense of endangerment that we find in the Gospel and letters of John. Perhaps, when today's Christianity does find itself a minority faith, as is the case now in some places in Africa and Asia and seems likely to become the case in parts of Europe and the Americas, it can find a new, more moderate language to express its relationship to the world. Yet perhaps there will also be times when lines must be drawn and a stand must be taken without compromise, and suffering endured without relief. Then the language of 1 John may come to seem all too appropriate once again.

Yet for all this sense of endangerment and oppression, the point being made here is that those who "belong to God" (the word "children," as in the NRSV of verse 19, is not actually in the Greek) are safe from the power of the evil one who controls the world (which, of course, includes the opponents; see 3:10, 12; 4:1–6). Those who belong to God, who maintain their faith in Jesus the Son of God, have conquered the evil one and his world, which is passing away (2:12–14, 17; 5:4–5). Terrifying as it may sound, verse 19 is meant to reassure the readers that, *even though* the whole world appears to lie in the power of evil, they belong to God who cannot be defeated. Thus they can have confidence, even in the face of seemingly overwhelming odds.

The ultimate foundation for this assurance is given in verse 20. This

final statement of what "we know" is the basis for the readers' confidence
as children of God who belong to God. Not surprisingly it is expressed in
terms of the coming of the Son of God, that is, "his Son Jesus Christ." The
use of this full title puts us in mind, for the final time, of the ending of the
Fourth Gospel (John 20:31), and of the understanding of the human Jesus
as the divine Christ and Son of God that has been so insistently defended
throughout 1 John (1:3; 2:22–24; 3:23; 4:2–3, 14–15; 5:1, 5, 6, 9–13). At
first sight, it even seems that the author identifies Jesus as "the true God
and eternal life." That would certainly be consistent with the Gospel of
John, which calls Jesus "God" (John 1:1, 18; 20:28) and identifies him with
life (John 1:3–4; 11:25; 14:6). However, earlier in the verse our author has
spoken twice of God as "the one who is true" and has clearly distinguished
this One from "his Son Jesus Christ." This suggests that "the true God"
does not after all refer to Jesus. The suggestion is confirmed when we look
at John 17:3: "And this is eternal life, that they may know you, the only
true God, and Jesus Christ whom you have sent." Knowing the true God
brings eternal life, and this knowledge comes in knowing Jesus Christ (see
John 14:7–11), who was sent by the true God. This seems to be the point
of 1 John 5:20 as well.

The purpose of Jesus' coming was to bring this knowledge of the true
God, that is, the God who is truth. Though 1 John is greatly concerned to
distinguish truth from falsehood, it also speaks of "truth" in the more fundamental sense that is typical of the Gospel of John, as the divine reality,
the reality of God that brings all other reality into existence. Jesus the Son
of God has come and has made God known (compare 4:9–10). That is, in
Jesus we have encountered the reality at the heart of the universe, and in
this encounter we have been given the very life by which that reality lives,
eternal life, the life of God. Indeed, in Jesus Christ, the Son of God, we are
actually *in God*, a claim that goes beyond even what the Gospel of John
says (see the comments on 1 John 3:24). Though it is Jesus who has made
this relationship possible, we now have in him a direct access to God, such
that (for those who believe in Jesus and love one another) we abide in God
and God abides in us (3:24; 4:12–16).

After all the subtlety, difficulty, and downright unclarity that 1 John has
had to offer, it is probably not surprising that it ends on a puzzling note,
to say the least. What have idols got to do with anything that the author
has been saying? Having spent so much time warning against his opponents' false teaching and lack of love, does he turn at the end to a completely unrelated warning against involvement with pagan religion? Or do
the "idols" stand for sin or deception in some general sense, not connected

to the opponents? Difficult though 1 John may be at times, neither of those explanations seems very likely. Somehow, the admonition "Little children, keep yourselves from idols" must be related to the overall thought of this writing and to its concluding verses in particular.

We may begin by asking very simply what an idol is. The word literally means an image, in a variety of senses. In Jewish usage, however (usage that was picked up by the early Christians), the idols or images of other gods, that is, the statues used in temples and shrines, had come to be identified with the gods themselves. This was probably not quite fair to the way in which the worshipers of those gods understood the function of the images; but the idea of "gods made by human hands," as developed in the Hebrew Bible (Deut. 4:28; 2 Kings 19:18; 22:17; 2 Chron. 32:19; Pss. 96:5; 97:7; 115:4–8; Jer. 1:16; 25:6; 44:8), became firmly fixed in both Jewish and Christian theology. Indeed, we find in Jewish texts, beginning in the Hebrew Bible (Jer. 10:1–16; Isa. 44:9–20), a kind of standard criticism of such gods, who are contrasted with the God of Israel, who is the true God, the living God (2 Kings 19:16; Jer. 10:10; note also Dan. 6:20, 26).

It is this traditional biblical contrast that causes our author to make reference to idols at the end of his writing. He has just identified the God made known by Jesus Christ as "the true God and eternal life," terms quite similar to the ones used to distinguish Israel's God from the idols. This distinction was important for Jewish people living in the pagan world of the Roman Empire. Jewish writers used it to defend their own religion against attacks from outsiders, to promote faithfulness among their fellow Jews, and to criticize the religion of pagans, some of whom were persuaded and became worshipers of "the living God." The earliest Christian missionaries to the Gentiles, including the apostle Paul, were Jews who had been brought up and educated in this environment and knew how to make use of this standard rhetoric. (Paul uses some of it in Rom. 1:18–32.) When preaching to Gentiles, their first task was often to convert them to faith in the one true God, and we find evidence of this, for instance, in Acts 14:15; 17:24–25 (note also 2 Cor. 6:16). The best example for our purposes is 1 Thessalonians 1:9: the Thessalonian Gentiles, when they became Christians, "turned to God from idols, to serve a living and true God." Many of the readers of 1 John had probably had a similar experience at their conversion, so that when the author reminded them that Jesus had brought knowledge of "the one who is true," "the true God and eternal life," they would have found it perfectly natural to think of "idols" as the opposite of this God.

If the opposite of the God revealed in Jesus Christ, the Son of God, is an idol, then this final verse does have meaning in terms of the battle that our author has been fighting throughout his text. The opponents did not acknowledge the human Jesus as the one in whom God was made known, nor did they acknowledge him as identical with the divine Christ and Son of God (2:22–23; 4:2–3; 5:9–12). But if indeed it was the human Jesus Christ, come in the flesh, who made known the God who is love (4:2, 9–10), "the true God and eternal life," then any God not revealed through him could only be an idol. "Little children, keep yourselves from idols" is a final warning to avoid the opponents, who apparently claimed that divine revelation took place only through a spiritual Christ, not through the human Jesus. Having already called them false prophets (4:1–3), the author naturally associates them with false gods, in whose names false prophets speak (Deut. 13:1–5; 18:20–22). Just as their teaching and their lack of love put them on the side of the world and the evil one, on the side of falsehood rather than truth, so their claims to know God, to abide in God, to be "in the light" (if such claims stand behind 1:6; 2:4, 6, 9) amount to no more than the delusions of idolatry.

To know the true God is to have eternal life (John 17:3), a life that comes from being born of God. No other god has the power to give life. Yet this God has chosen to give eternal life through a human death; the God whom no one has ever seen has chosen to be made known in "what we have heard, what we have seen with our eyes, what we have looked at and touched with our hands" (1 John 1:1)—in a mortal man, Jesus. However much there may be within 1 John that is simply inconsistent, this claim is the genuine paradox of Christianity, expressed most sharply in the Gospel of John and interpreted here in a situation where some had threatened to dissolve the paradox by denying the physical means of divine salvation and revelation. "The Word became flesh" (John 1:14); and so 1 John can say, "the eternal life that was with the Father was revealed to us" (1 John 1:2) in the person of Jesus Christ who has come in the flesh (4:2); and "God's love was revealed among us in this way: God sent his only Son into the world so that we might live through him" (4:9); and "we know love by this, that he laid down his life for us—and we ought to lay down our lives for one another" (3:16). Life through death, God made known in mortal flesh—it is not an easy claim to understand or to maintain and promote. But 1 John will not let us back away from it into some idolatry of our own making, not even an idolatry of the spirit. There is perhaps only one way to enter into this strange paradox and live in it so that both we and the world can see it as divine truth. And that way is: "Beloved, let us love one another."

Second John

Introduction

What little there is to say about the structure of 2 John can be found in the commentary on it. Unlike 1 John, it is a genuine letter in its format, but it is not simply a personal note. Rather, it is intended to convey something of the elder's authority and to encourage its readers to take certain actions.

Not much needs to be said about the setting of 2 John either, since it seems to be identical with that of 1 John. Here again we encounter the new commandment to love one another, and the deceiver and antichrist who does not properly confess Jesus Christ. Though a few scholars have proposed, on the basis of a minute examination of its language, that 2 John addresses some other set of circumstances, it seems most reasonable to take it at face value. Therefore the necessary information regarding the controversy behind 2 John can be found in the Introduction to 1 John and need not be repeated here. Indeed, since 2 John seems to be not much more than a summary of 1 John, we are faced with the question why this little letter was written at all.

Perhaps a clue for answering this question can be found in one feature of 2 John that sets it apart from 1 John. Like 1 John, this letter seeks to persuade its readers not to fall in with the opponents' ideas about Jesus or with their lack of love; but it adds a specific course of action for the readers to follow: refusal to take in traveling teachers who spread these ideas, in order not to provide a base of operations for their mission. (For details regarding the issue of hospitality, see the commentary on 2 John.) Perhaps, then, the elder is addressing this letter to members of the community in another town, to let them know of the danger (as he sees it), and urge them to take preventive measures against the expansion of the opponents' influence. It is also conceivable that 2 John is actually earlier than 1 John (the Johannine letters, like those of Paul, are arranged by length, not chronology), and represents a quick note, a kind of stopgap, to have something in place until the elder could compose a more thorough exhortation.

RESISTING THE ANTICHRIST
2 John

In some ways, 2 John seems almost like a summary of 1 John, and it may have been written in the same situation (see the Introduction, which also discusses the purpose for the writing of 2 John). Here, as in 1 John, we find the two commandments to believe in Jesus and love one another, but compressed together in such a way as to make their relationship very difficult to grasp. Because 2 John is so brief and so condensed, we are almost forced to use 1 John to interpret it, even though we can't be completely sure that they refer to exactly the same issues. On the other hand, unlike 1 John, 2 John closely resembles the standard format used for a one-page Greek letter in ancient times. It begins by naming the sender and the recipients, then affirms divine blessing on both and expresses joy at the recipients' well-being (vv. 1–4). The body of the letter is found in verses 5–11, then the writer concludes by looking forward to personal contact and sending greetings from others (vv. 12–13). (Although the NRSV and most other English translations begin the body with verse 4, the content of that verse is more typical of the *openings* of ancient letters, while "But now . . . I ask you" in verse 5 was a common way of starting the body. The theme of "truth" also connects verse 4 to verses 1–3.) These three parts—the opening, the body, and the closing of the letter—give us a framework for examining 2 John.

Greetings to the Elect Lady (2 John 1–4)

1 **The elder to the elect lady and her children, whom I love in the truth, and not only I but also all who know the truth,** 2 **because of the truth that abides in us and will be with us forever:**

3 **Grace, mercy, and peace will be with us from God the Father and from Jesus Christ, the Father's Son, in truth and love.**

4 **I was overjoyed to find some of your children walking in the truth, just as we have been commanded by the Father.**

As I indicated above, 2 John uses the basic opening format of a standard Greek letter. However, the elder modified this format in order to make his letter more official than a purely personal, private one. The standard opening salutation "X to Y" (compare Acts 15:23; 23:26) has been greatly expanded in verses 1–2 with theological statements centering on "truth" (James 1:1 shows less extensive modifications). Verse 3 not only expresses an expectation of divine blessing, but does so in explicitly Christian terms, using a formula very much like the words "Grace to you and peace from God our Father and the Lord Jesus Christ" that we find in the letters of Paul (see Rom. 1:7; 1 Cor. 1:3; 2 Cor. 1:2) and among his followers (for the addition of "mercy," see especially 1 Tim. 1:2; 2 Tim. 1:2). The statement of joy at the recipients' well-being in verse 4 continues the theological theme of "truth"; it also provides a transition to the body of the letter by introducing the ideas of walking and of God's commandment. The original readers of 2 John would thus have found themselves looking at a document whose layout was familiar to them, whether from everyday letters or from other early Christian official letters, thus helping them to see quickly where the writer was going.

What may we learn from these opening sentences? The author calls himself "the elder," which was a common early Christian title. However, he uses it in an unusual way, since elsewhere we always read of "elders" in the plural, not of a single authority called "*the* elder" (see the Introduction to this volume for more discussion of the author's identity). He is writing to "the elect lady," which could refer to another church official. However, the fact that the author always uses a plural "you" in speaking to the recipients (vv. 6, 8, 10, 12), as well as the language of verse 13, suggests that "elect lady" is a symbolic term for a Christian congregation, whose members are called her "children." The word "elect" might also be translated "chosen"; it implies that the "lady" and her "sister" have been specially chosen to be God's people.

As a chosen body, the readers (like the author) have "the truth" or reality of God abiding in them. Since this divine truth will be with them forever, the author is able not merely to wish or pray that grace, mercy, and peace *may* be with them, but to assert confidently that this too *will* be with them. "Grace, mercy, peace" (there is no "and" in the Greek) is essentially treated as a single item. As noted above, it is a standard phrase in early Christian letters, so there is no point in trying to work out distinct meanings for each of the terms here. This grace-mercy-peace will be with the author and the readers "in truth and love," which may be a kind of shorthand for the two commandments promoted by the letters of John: true belief in Jesus and love for one another (1 John 3:23). It is in the keeping of these commandments that the chosenness of the people is visible (compare John 13:35) and that "grace-mercy-peace" will be with them.

"Truth," that is, a right understanding of the identity of Jesus Christ, is particularly important in 2 John. Indeed, these first four verses are thick with references to "truth," suggesting that the elder is making a very strong claim that he and the "lady," the congregation to whom he sent this letter, really do stand firm in this truth about Jesus. Because 2 John is primarily concerned to call the readers to the defense of this truth against the "deceivers" who have a different belief, the term "truth" itself takes on a sense that has less to do with the ultimate reality of God (its usual meaning in the Gospel of John) and more to do with the particular understanding of Jesus held by the elder and his party. Perhaps it might be more accurate to say that for the elder this understanding of Jesus *is* the truest expression of divine reality.

The author does not say how he has found some of the "children" of the "lady" walking in the truth. (There may be a bit of an ominous note in the word "some," suggesting that others are not walking in truth, that is, living in accordance with the truth.) Perhaps he has recently paid a visit to the congregation, or perhaps he has simply heard reports of their faithfulness. In any case, by expressing his joy at how well they are doing, the elder suggests that he and they are on the same side in the conflict with the "deceivers," and thus helps to assure a favorable hearing for his message.

Be on Guard against the Deceivers (2 John 5–11)

⁵ But now, dear lady, I ask you, not as though I were writing you a new commandment, but one we have had from the beginning, let us love one another. ⁶ And this is love, that we walk according to his commandments; this is the commandment just as you have heard it from the beginning—you must walk in it.

7 Many deceivers have gone out into the world, those who do not confess that Jesus Christ has come in the flesh; any such person is the deceiver and the antichrist! ⁸ Be on your guard, so that you do not lose what we have worked for, but may receive a full reward. ⁹ Everyone who does not abide in the teaching of Christ, but goes beyond it, does not have God; whoever abides in the teaching has both the Father and the Son. ¹⁰ Do not receive into the house or welcome anyone who comes to you and does not bring this teaching; ¹¹ for to welcome is to participate in the evil deeds of such a person.

The body of the letter begins with a reminder of the commandment to love one another. The statement that this is not a new commandment, but "one we have had from the beginning," is very similar to 1 John 2:7–8, which echoes John 13:34. Unlike those two passages, however, this verse only emphasizes the traditional nature of the commandment, not its newness (see comments on 1 John 2:7–8). Loving one another (that is, other Christians; see comments on 1 John 2:10) is not a new idea; it is what they have been taught ever since they became Christians. The elder simply wants them to put this into practice. And yet, as we will see, 2 John itself presents some difficult questions about how this commandment that believers "have had from the beginning" really is to be carried out.

Immediately after referring to this commandment to love one another, the author apparently gives an explanation of what this love means. Unfortunately, verse 6 presents the kind of tangle of Greek syntax that this writer so often seems to fall into—see, for example, 1 John 3:19–20. As in the case of that passage, it may be useful to compare several English translations that have different renderings of this verse, for instance, the New Revised Standard Version (given above), the *New International Version*, and the *Revised English Bible*. The NRSV translation, it seems to me, leaves unclear what is meant by "the commandment"; on the whole, I think that the REB straightens out the tangle in the clearest and most natural manner. I would offer the following as my own paraphrase of verse 6: "And love means that we should walk according to God's commandments. *That* is the meaning of the love commandment, just as you have heard from the beginning that you should walk in it."

Somewhat surprisingly, then, the first thing that the elder says about the meaning of the commandment to love one another is that it means walking (that is, living) in accordance with God's commandments in general. Of course, as I noted above, the letters of John (like the Gospel of John) present us with only two commandments, to believe in Jesus and to love one another. It seems then that our author is saying that keeping the latter commandment involves keeping the former as well. One way in which Christians show their love for one another is by believing in Jesus as the divine Son of God revealed in human flesh. The reasoning (to the extent that it can be clearly discerned) is similar to that in 1 John 5:1–2 (see comments there). If we are going to love our fellow-believers, then we must be faithful to the God whose children we all are; and our faithfulness means accepting the self-revelation that God has made in the manner in which God has chosen to make it—namely, in Jesus, the Messiah, the Son of God, fully divine and yet fully human. In fact, since it was in the human Jesus and his painful, all-too-human death that God made known what love really is, we cannot expect to love one another in the fullest sense if we do not acknowledge the revelation of God's love in Jesus Christ as the standard for our love, and indeed as its very source. Thus, beginning with the commandment to love one another, the elder moves quickly to the heart of his message: belief in Jesus' full humanity must be maintained at all costs.

Against whom must this belief be defended? Against the "deceivers," the "antichrists" who are promoting a different belief, one that sees Jesus as too divine to be fully human. The language used to state the elder's case in 2 John 7–9 is again very much like that of 1 John, and I need not repeat here the comments on 1 John 2:18–27 and 4:1–3, to which you should refer at this point. The similarity suggests that the opponents are the same people, promoting the same beliefs, even though 2 John, brief as it is, does not mention everything that 1 John does (for instance, the "last hour" or the testing of spirits). There is one noteworthy difference between the two letters, which unfortunately cannot be seen in the NRSV translation. First John 4:2 speaks of "Jesus Christ having come in the flesh"; 2 John 7 literally speaks of "Jesus Christ *coming* in the flesh." Scholars have made a number of suggestions about the significance of this variation. Yet the difference does not seem great enough to show that 2 John is addressing a problem very much different from the one addressed by 1 John. Both writings seem to be concerned that their readers not fall prey to a conception of Christ that regards him simply as divine and not truly human, or at any rate one that does not see his humanity as playing a significant part in his work of salvation.

The elder does add some new features in his treatment of this issue in 2 John. For one thing, he warns the readers to be careful not to lose what "we" (that is, the whole community) have worked for. There is a reward to be gained by being faithful to the teaching that they have received, an idea that is more typical of other New Testament writings than it is of the Gospel of John and 1 John (for example, Matt. 6:1–6; Heb. 10:35). The reward is not specified, but one would naturally think of the eternal life emphasized throughout John and 1 John as coming through faith in Jesus. This life is received by those who believe that Jesus is the Messiah, the Son of God; they have already passed from death to life, and they will be raised to life on the last day (John 3:14–16; 5:24; 6:40, 47, 54; 11:25–27; 20:31; 1 John 2:24–25; 5:10–13). If this is what the elder is thinking of here, he emphasizes the future reception of life as a reward on the last day rather than the present possession of it, which is the focus of the Gospel of John.

Even so, however, the reward is not something earned by good conduct, but something that comes through belief in the fleshly, human reality of Jesus Christ. The elder refers to letting go of this belief as "going beyond" the teaching instead of "abiding" in it. The choice was apparently between sticking with what the readers had been taught about Jesus "from the beginning" and going forward into the new teaching being offered by the opponents. The elder's insistence on "abiding" and his claim that "going forward" is not "walking in truth" but "deceiving" could be understood as an absolute prohibition on any kind of progress in Christian thinking. However, "progress" as we understand it was a concept almost completely unknown in the age when 2 John was written. People did not have an expectation that life would continually get better, whether in a material sense or in a social, cultural, or political one. Stability was the norm and the ideal, and change and innovation were often looked on with suspicion. In their first several centuries of existence, Christians were constantly faced with the accusation of being *new*, of abandoning the traditions of their ancestors and of their culture as a whole. In a sense, it is actually this newness, this break with cultural traditions, that the elder is seeking to maintain here. The opponents' claim that the Christ must be purely divine, above the ordinary conditions of human life, in order to bring a heavenly salvation was one that would have made sense in many quarters of that society, where hope for salvation was often a hope to escape the body and its limitations into a realm of pure spirit. This is why our author sees the opponents' teaching—discarding the claim that salvation comes in the human Jesus—as giving in to "the world's" way of thinking (see 1 John 4:2–5). Part of the newness of Christianity was its claim that a divine Savior could bring eternal life by dying a cruel human death, and the elder resists any move to abandon that unique position. To be sure, he does so in a way that seems to share the ancient world's emphasis on maintaining traditions. He does not speak of abiding in Jesus or in God, as we find in 1 John (2:24, 27, 28; 3:6, 24; 4:12, 15–16), but of abiding in a *teaching*, that is, in a doctrine. Yet even though the elder speaks against "going forward" or "going beyond" the original teaching, it might equally well be said that the opponents' position represented a "going backward" into a less radically different theological and philosophical stance.

The elder is seeking to guard the distinctiveness, the newness, of Christian belief against a retreat into a more commonplace understanding that saw flesh as unable to bring about divine salvation. He, does so, however, in words that in themselves sound like a retreat from newness. Perhaps we may see some parallels in our own times, when people debate whether Christianity is something radically new or something deeply traditional. Is it a break with the past in order to forge new ways of living out God's will for the human race, or is it a means of preserving longstanding beliefs, values, and customs? Second John seems to offer evidence to support both sides of this debate, which may indicate that both impulses are authentic features of Christianity. It may also suggest that one of the most difficult things about Christianity, which began as a movement of newness and creativity of the spirit, is to find ways of preserving new insights once they have become traditional. How can our religion manage to preserve the freshness and distinctiveness of its beliefs and way of life, without either falling apart into fads and meaningless innovations or falling back into cultural traditionalism or falling down into a closed-minded and narrow dogmatism? Second John may not give us a very clear answer to this question, but it does help us to focus on the need for asking it.

There is one other way in which the treatment of the opponents in 2 John differs from that in 1 John. The author proposes a specific course of action for the readers to take to prevent the opponents from making inroads into their community: "Do not receive into the house or welcome anyone who comes to you and does not bring this teaching." This sounds like a remarkably harsh mandate, especially from a writer who has just been urging his readers, "let us love one another"! In order to understand what the elder is requesting here, we need to understand something about the nature of hospitality in the early church and the way in which early Christians conducted their missionary ventures.

The earliest Christian gatherings for worship, of course, were not held in special church buildings but in people's homes (see, for example, Acts 12:12; Rom. 16:5; 1 Cor. 16:19; Col. 4:15; Philemon 2). This meant that the people hosting the church in their house were not only showing hospitality, but helping to make the Christian mission possible. When the church spread into new territories, the homes of converts often became centers not only for worship but for the work of evangelization. When apostles, teachers, and other workers in the church traveled to a city where a Christian community already existed, they sought lodging not in inns but in believers' homes. To receive such travelers into one's house meant furnishing a base for their work: a place to stay, something to eat, perhaps a forum in which to address a congregation. Hospitality of this sort was a major expression of Christian love, but it was also a significant means of spreading and strengthening the Christian faith. Various texts in the New Testament and elsewhere show how this worked. (See, for example, Acts 10:5–6; 16:14–15; 18:1–7; 20:20–21; 21:8, 16; 28:14; Rom. 15:23–24; 16:1–2; Titus 3:13; and for the roots of this practice in the mission of Jesus, see Mark 6:10; Luke 10:5–7.) Hospitality to travelers on mission also forms a major theme in 3 John.

This is the context in which we need to see the prohibition in 2 John 10–11. The opponents no doubt sought to spread their teaching in the same way as others in the early church. By forbidding hospitality to them, the elder hoped to hinder this spread, "for to welcome is to participate in the evil deeds of such a person." That is exactly how things worked in the early Christian "network." To welcome someone, that is, to show them hospitality, was to offer support to them and their work, in a way that did indeed mean participating in their preaching, teaching, or mission. Since the elder regarded the work of the opponents as evil, offering them hospitality likewise meant sharing in this evil. The point was not to snub the opponents socially, nor to be hard-hearted toward them, but to prevent the expansion of their teaching (compare Rom. 16:17–18). Just as hospitality was both an expression of love and a mission strategy, the elder's forbidding of hospitality was not so much a refusal of love (though it's hard to deny that it was that also) as it was a strategy to thwart the mission of the opponents. Surprisingly (or perhaps not so surprisingly), in 3 John it appears that a similar method was also used *against* the elder!

In some ways, this strategy has a remarkably contemporary flavor. Most people are familiar with the boycott—a refusal to engage in business or other dealings—as a means of pressuring an organization to change its ways. This tactic has often been used successfully in civil rights and other causes; you may even have participated in one. What the elder is advocating is a kind of boycott of the opponents' mission. Similar actions sometimes take place in Christian denominations today. Particular individuals, or even an entire congregation, may disagree with the direction the denomination is taking and refuse to contribute their full financial support. Sometimes the process goes in the other direction, with denominational authorities expelling a congregation that has, in their opinion, broken with denominational doctrine, practice, or tradition. You may be able to think of one or more such instances in your own denomination. "Hot-button" issues—current ones include homosexuality and the role of women in the church—are especially likely to lead to such actions. Sometimes the hope is that enough pressure will be generated to cause the other side to rethink their position; sometimes people simply feel that it would be morally wrong to "participate in the evil deeds" of the other party.

People tend to favor or criticize such a strategy depending on how they feel about the issue in question. A person might consider such a "boycott" the only morally viable alternative in one case, and a lamentable breakdown of Christian love and unity in another! The same is liable to be true of our responses to 2 John. If we feel that doctrinal precision and correctness is something to be guarded at all costs, then the elder's move may seem absolutely necessary and a valid precedent for similar actions today. If we feel that doctrinal questions sometimes get in the way of the love and worship that are at the heart of Christianity, we may find the elder's measures regrettable. Either way, though, we are forced to recognize that divisions, conflicts, and highly charged politics were a factor already in the earliest days of the Christian church. Whether we find this intriguing, exciting, or dismaying, it is at least a reminder that the challenges and discord facing the church in our time are nothing new. Christianity has faced, and survived, such problems practically since its beginning, and it will surely survive our contemporary disagreements.

Conclusion (2 John 12–13)

12 **Although I have much to write to you, I would rather not use paper and ink; instead I hope to come to you and talk with you face to face, so that our joy may be complete.**
   13 **The children of your elect sister send you their greetings.**

The final sentences of 2 John express ideas and feelings that were often placed at the end of a Greek letter in ancient times: greetings from those at a distance, a preference for personal contact over mere letter-writing, and a hope for the pleasure of that contact in the near future. The conclusion of 3 John is very similar. (For final greetings, compare also Rom. 16:3–16, 21–23; 1 Cor. 16:19–21; Phil. 4:21–22; Col. 4:10–18; 2 Tim. 4:19–21; Titus 3:15; Heb. 13:24; 1 Peter 5:13.) Some of the language that the elder uses, however, is particular to the Gospel and letters of John. Specifically, the hope that "our joy may be complete" in a future visit reminds us of 1 John 1:4, and also of John 3:29; 15:11; 16:24; 17:13. Usually this expression refers to the ultimate, divine joy of the relationship between Jesus and his disciples, not to the more everyday joy of a simple visit. Perhaps the elder means to hint that even such pleasures, among believers, are a foretaste of the joy to come.

Third John

Introduction

As with 2 John, the few remarks necessary for understanding the structure of 3 John are found in the commentary that follows. Third John is the clearest example in the New Testament of a simple personal letter and it tends to use the standard language of such letters (and of the early Christian mission), rather than the words and phrases that are typical of the Gospel and the other letters of John. Yet even 3 John is not just about personal matters but has "business" to attend to. As in the other two Johannine letters, the business involves a controversy within a Christian community. It is tempting to assume that this is the same controversy as in the other two letters. Yet there is nothing in 3 John about proper belief in Jesus, nor does the elder call his opponent here an "antichrist" or a deceiver. Third John probably deals with a situation entirely unconnected to the controversy behind 1 and 2 John. At any rate, if there is a connection, it does not appear in this letter.

What are the issues in 3 John then? They have to do with the "church" (a term found only here in the Gospel and letters of John) and with hospitality shown to traveling missionaries and teachers. In fact, this hospitality is really the major issue in 3 John. The controversy only surfaces in relation to the need for hospitality, and we need to be careful not to focus too much of our attention on it. The significance of hospitality in relation to the mission of the early church is discussed in my commentary on 2 John as well as in that on 3 John. Suffice it to say here that without hospitality shown to travelers, Christianity would not have spread as it did in its earliest decades. Third John was written mainly to encourage its recipient, Gaius, to continue to show the kind of hospitality that he had shown in the past. In connection with this exhortation, 3 John also serves as a letter of recommendation for the travelers (in particular a man named Demetrius) whom the elder wishes Gaius to assist.

One reason why Gaius' hospitality has become so important is that someone else, named Diotrephes, no longer welcomes the elder's messengers.

Scholars have spent a great deal of effort trying to understand the nature of the controversy between the elder and Diotrephes. Some have suggested that Diotrephes was one of the heretics whom the elder opposes in 1 and 2 John, but there is no indication of that. Some have turned the tables and proposed that Diotrephes considered the elder to be a heretic and was trying to keep his teaching from infecting Diotrephes' own church, or that Diotrephes was simply trying to keep all traveling teachers out of his church in order to avoid any kind of doctrinal danger. This goes well beyond anything that 3 John actually says. What it does say is that Diotrephes "likes to put himself first over them"—that is, over the members of the church, perhaps a house church that met in his home. This suggests that the issue is one of authority, or maybe just power. The territorial authority of bishops was just beginning to develop about the time that 3 John was written, and some scholars have suggested that Diotrephes was trying to assert this authority against the elder, whose own authority was a kind of relic from an earlier system. Others have suggested that the elder himself was trying to wield the authority of a bishop or something similar. But 3 John does not use the term bishop and does not suggest that either Diotrephes or the elder was seeking jurisdiction over the other. Diotrephes was able to expel members of his congregation who offered hospitality to messengers from the elder, but beyond that he could only use "evil words" against him. The elder, meanwhile, also has nothing but words to use against Diotrephes. Thus it is not clear that either of these men could hope to exercise any concrete authority against the other.

In fact, unclarity may be the most certain characteristic of this situation! It took some time for systematic structures of authority to develop in the Christian churches, and 3 John comes from a community that may have resisted such structures in any case. (Note 1 John 2:27, and the equality within the church implied by the language of "brothers and sisters" throughout these letters.) This very absence of clear structures may have encouraged the development of power struggles such as the one between Diotrephes and the elder. In a Christian community that may not have done much theological thinking about authority, people seeking to exercise it were to a certain extent groping in the dark. It is no wonder that we feel somewhat the same way when we try to understand this controversy.

Where does Gaius come into all this? He was evidently not a member of Diotrephes' congregation and was in a position to offer hospitality to traveling teachers, missionaries, and others. The elder does not ask him to intervene in Diotrephes' church or to do anything directly regarding Diotrephes at all. Though he seems to have been annoyed with Diotrephes, the elder appears confident that he can deal with him on his own. He is also confident of his relationship with Gaius, which seems to be a warm one. With the urging of this little letter, the elder expects Gaius to take care of the needs of the travelers and so continue to be a "co-worker with the truth," that is, be someone who does his share to promote the mission of Christianity. Third John thus gives us an intriguing look at some of the ways in which that mission worked in the early days and some of the internal obstacles it could have to face.

HOSPITALITY AND AUTHORITY
3 John

Third John is unique among the letters of the New Testament in that it seems to be a genuinely personal letter, rather than one intended for reading to a congregation (even Philemon is also addressed "to the church in your house"), or for establishing certain practices in the church (like the letters to Timothy and Titus). Its format is simply that of an ordinary Greek letter, without the adaptations for more official purposes found even in 2 John (see the comments on 2 John). The only thing missing is the customary "Greetings" at the beginning (see Acts 15:23; 23:26; James 1:1) or a modified form such as that found in 2 John 3; and "Farewell" at the end (see Acts 15:29). The letter falls easily into three sections, each beginning with the word "Beloved" addressed to its recipient (vv. 2, 5, 11).

Like many letters, it was written in response to a particular situation. Of course, that situation was well known to the original writer and recipient, so that the writer did not need to include much of the detailed information that would make the situation clear to us. For a fuller discussion of the problems of understanding this situation see the Introduction to 3 John. Here let me only repeat that the letter was written by someone who calls himself simply "the elder" to a man named Gaius, requesting that Gaius receive some Christian travelers, apparently messengers from the elder, with hospitality. The elder's messengers had already been refused hospitality by someone named Diotrephes, for reasons that are not very clear but are apparently related to some kind of power struggle between him and the elder. This power struggle was set in the context of the mission of the early church, a context that is reflected in several terms that are found only in 3 John among the Gospel and letters of John: the word "church," "send on," "for the sake of the name," and "co-workers" (all in vv. 6–10). These terms will be discussed in the comments that follow.

Opening (3 John 1–4)

1 The elder to the beloved Gaius, whom I love in truth.

2 Beloved, I pray that all may go well with you and that you may be in good health, just as it is well with your soul. ³ I was overjoyed when some of the friends arrived and testified to your faithfulness to the truth, namely how you walk in the truth. ⁴ I have no greater joy than this, to hear that my children are walking in the truth.

The letter begins in the usual way, with the name of sender and recipient. (Regarding the identity of the elder, see the Introduction to this volume. Nothing else is known about Gaius.) The added words "whom I love in truth" use language typical of the letters of John (see 1 John 3:18 and 2 John 1). The prayers and compliments in verses 2–4 are the kind of thing expected in a Greek letter opening. However, the references to Gaius' soul and to his walking in the truth reflect the specifically Christian and religious character of 3 John. "Walking in the truth" is again typical of these letters (2 John 4). Indeed, "truth" (the NRSV adds the idea of "faithfulness") is a major theme not only in the letters but in the Gospel of John, where it refers to the reality of God manifested in Jesus (John 1:14, 17; 8:31–32, 40; 14:6; 17:17–19; 18:37). In 2 John, "walking in the truth" seems to mean persisting in the true teaching about Jesus. Here, however, the "truth" of Gaius means not his beliefs but his actions, his love, since that is what the "friends" have specifically attested (v. 6). This love has been shown in his hospitality to the Christian brothers and sisters who are traveling on mission, a hospitality that makes Gaius a co-worker with the truth (vv. 5–8). (The NRSV translates the Greek word that means "brothers" or "brothers and sisters" as "friends" in 3 John; this is unfortunate, as it must then use the same term for the word that actually does mean "friends" in verse 15.) The elder loves Gaius in truth, and Gaius walks in the truth by loving his fellow-believers. Thus even this relatively "non-theological" little letter reminds us that the truth revealed in Jesus is that God is love (1 John 4:7–16) and that we "walk" in this truth when we actively love one another.

Gaius's Hospitality and Diotrephes' Inhospitality (3 John 5–10)

5 Beloved, you do faithfully whatever you do for the friends, even though they are strangers to you; ⁶ they have testified to your love before the church. You will do well to send them on in a manner worthy of God; ⁷ for they began their journey for the sake of Christ, accepting no support from non-believers. ⁸ Therefore

we ought to support such people, so that we may become co-workers with the truth.

9 I have written something to the church; but Diotrephes, who likes to put himself first, does not acknowledge our authority. 10 So if I come, I will call attention to what he is doing in spreading false charges against us. And not content with those charges, he refuses to welcome the friends, and even prevents those who want to do so and expels them from the church.

Again addressing Gaius as "beloved," the elder now turns to the substance of his letter. The language of verses 5–8 is somewhat indirect, so that it might not be immediately apparent to the modern reader what the elder is asking of Gaius. Phrases like "you do faithfully whatever you do" and "you will do well to . . ." were commonly used as polite ways of asking a favor, especially in letters of recommendation. Such letters were used a great deal in the ancient world, but not as part of an application for a job or some other position as we use them. Rather, they were used to introduce unknown travelers ("strangers," as v. 5 says), who might show up at one's doorstep with a letter from a friend vouching for their good character and their need of help. Romans 16:1–2 and 2 Corinthians 8:16–24 are other examples of letters of recommendation in the New Testament (see also Acts 18:27; 1 Cor. 16:3; 2 Cor. 3:1). The elder is thus introducing certain Christian brothers (or brothers and sisters; "friends" in the NRSV) to Gaius, and asking him to show them hospitality. These brothers (and perhaps Demetrius [v. 12] in particular) would have been carrying 3 John with them as their letter of recommendation.

These brothers and sisters are traveling "for the sake of Christ," literally, "for the sake of the name," that is, the name of Jesus. Though the expression "the name" is found only in Acts 5:41 elsewhere in the New Testament, "the name of Jesus" (or "this name") is often used in the book of Acts in connection with the early church's evangelizing mission (Acts 4:17–18; 5:28, 40; 8:12; 9:27). The reference here is surely also to mission, whether evangelization or mission of some other kind. For this reason, the travelers seek aid only from other Christians, not from non-believers (literally "Gentiles," a term for outsiders that the church inherited from its Jewish origins). The elder asks Gaius specifically to "support" them, which refers to material aid such as shelter and food. He also asks him to "send them on," which means to give them concrete assistance as they journey on from Gaius's town (Acts 15:3; Rom. 15:24; 1 Cor. 16:6, 11; 2 Cor. 1:16; Titus 3:13). Hospitality such as this was not only a means of helping out others in need, but was vitally important to the maintenance and progress of the Christian mission (see further the comments on 2 John 10–11). People who offered such hospitality were "co-workers with the truth," just like the mission travelers themselves—"co-workers" is a term that Paul often uses to refer to those who labored with him in spreading the gospel (for example, 1 Cor. 16:16; 2 Cor. 8:23; Phil. 2:25; 4:3; 1 Thess. 3:2; Philemon 1, 24). Gaius has already shown hospitality in this manner on previous occasions (vv. 3, 6), and the elder needs him to repeat it now, especially since someone else has refused such cooperation.

This inhospitable person was Diotrephes, about whom nothing is known other than what we read in 3 John. Messengers from the elder had come to "the church," presumably meaning the household congregation over which Diotrephes was seeking to exert authority, and Diotrephes had refused to receive them or the letter they carried. Further, he had expelled those who did receive them from the church. We have no way of knowing exactly what lay behind this conflict. Diotrephes may have been the host of the house church in question and may have been trying to use that position to exercise a new level of authority over it. According to the elder, at any rate, he "likes to put himself first *over them*" (the last two words are in the Greek, but omitted in the NRSV). Perhaps he had some specific reason for hostility to the elder as well, but if so the elder never mentions it. This is about as much as we know for certain about the conflict, but several aspects of it can be addressed further here (other details are in the Introduction to 3 John).

The brothers and sisters (NRSV "friends") whom Diotrephes refused to welcome may or may not have been the same as the ones whom the elder urges Gaius to receive hospitably, and they may have been on the same mission or a different one. We also do not know the content of the letter they carried from the elder to the church; it could have been 2 John, but there is no particular reason to think so. Diotrephes had refused to give them a welcome and in so doing he had also refused to welcome the elder. The same word for "welcome" is used in both verse 9 and verse 10, although the NRSV, printed above, translates it "acknowledge our authority" in verse 9. It probably just means "welcome," however, so that it is not clear that the dispute really had to do with authority, whether that of the elder or that of Diotrephes. The elder speaks of it as a matter of welcoming—that is, of hospitality.

Diotrephes not only refused to offer this hospitality, but he prevented others from doing so as well. "Expelling them from the church" is not necessarily the same as what came to be called "excommunication" in later times. "The church" here likely means a single congregation, as it commonly does in Paul's letters. It does not refer to the entire church as an institution; that level of organization had not yet emerged. Nevertheless, Diotrephes prevented those who offered hospitality to the elder's messengers from meeting with the congregation, and that would have been a serious blow in a small, tightly-knit community. It would have been all the more so if this community, like the ones visible elsewhere in the Gospel and letters of John, felt itself to be rather alienated from "the world" outside (see John 7:7; 14:17, 19; 15:18–25; 17:14–16; 1 John 3:1, 13; 4:4–6; 5:19). Moreover, Diotrephes' prevention of hospitality is reminiscent of the instructions given by the elder himself in 2 John 10–11. As was the case in 2 John, Diotrephes' aim may have been to prevent the elder from spreading his teaching by hindering the messengers he sent. However, this hindrance may also simply have been a by-product of a conflict whose real causes lay elsewhere.

Besides the refusal of hospitality and of the elder's letter, Diotrephes has also been "spreading false charges" against the elder. The Greek expression is actually more vivid: "babbling against us with evil words." This suggests that whatever Diotrephes was saying about the elder was both vicious and ridiculous. We may wonder, of course, if Diotrephes would have described the elder's words in 3 John in the same way!

As in 2 John, we see here that church politics is not at all a new development. Whatever may have been the exact issue that caused the conflict between the elder and Diotrephes, the result was a battle that involved others who may have been perfectly innocent, perhaps even uninterested in the conflict. Third John probably comes from a time when precise lines of authority had not yet been established in the church overall, so that individuals who saw either a need for church discipline or an opportunity for self-promotion could step into a power vacuum and try to take charge.

Eventually, the church developed a system of bishops wielding authority over defined geographical areas—indeed, this development was taking place during the very period when 3 John was probably written. This system has continued in the Orthodox, Roman Catholic, and some Protestant traditions, while other Protestant bodies have devised different methods of organization. Any such method will have its own strengths and weaknesses. Third John probably shows us a situation wherein a loose, unstructured system, which allowed for a great deal of freedom, both for individuals and for local congregations, was beginning to show signs of strain at its weak points. These strains had implications not only for leaders but for mission workers and for ordinary Christians as well. As is so often the case, when the higher-ups do battle the fallout rains down on the people below. Christians who simply sought to go on mission for "the name" and others who wished to be "co-workers with the truth" found their sincere efforts hampered by power struggles going on above. The picture is not a pretty one and it may hold a warning that is as relevant for the church today as it was in ancient times.

The elder plans to deal with Diotrephes in person on a future visit. In the meantime, he can still carry out his plans, if only Gaius will receive "the brothers and sisters" hospitably. He seems to be informing Gaius of the situation regarding Diotrephes simply in order to "bring him up to speed" on the subject; having done so, he can turn to one final request.

Demetrius's Good Example (3 John 11–12)

11 Beloved, do not imitate what is evil but imitate what is good. Whoever does good is from God; whoever does evil has not seen God. 12 Everyone has testified favorably about Demetrius, and so has the truth itself. We also testify for him, and you know that our testimony is true.

Moral exhortation in the ancient world, like that in many cultures, made much use of examples, both good ones to be imitated and bad ones to be avoided. Clearly Diotrephes represents a bad example for the elder, who urges Gaius not to be like him. For a good example, he holds up Demetrius, another otherwise-unknown individual. (Of course, Gaius himself is his own good example in verses 3–8.) So little is actually said about Demetrius, however, that it is hard for us to know just how Gaius is supposed to imitate his example. Another possibility is that the elder's purpose is to commend Demetrius to Gaius's hospitality, perhaps as the individual who carried 3 John to Gaius (there was no postal service in ancient times), one of the "brothers" or "brothers and sisters" (NRSV "friends") commended as a group in verses 5–8 (compare Rom. 16:1–2). Gaius can feel confident, then, in offering aid and support to Demetrius, who is well attested by all.

The elder uses some rather heavy-duty language for such relatively mundane purposes. The assertion that "the truth itself" has testified favorably about Demetrius suggests an attestation with a divine source of some kind, though it could also mean (among other things) that his manner of life is in accord with the truth (as is the case with Gaius, according to verses 3–4). "You know that our testimony is true" is based on John 5:31–32; 19:35; 21:24, where the subject is testimony to Jesus Christ. It is hard to know whether it is the intensity of the situation, or of the elder himself, or of this particular group of Christians that causes such highly theological language to be used for a mere human recommendation; or whether what we find here is a late stage in the use of such language, when the terminology itself was becoming trivialized into slogans.

Conclusion (3 John 13–15)

13 **I have much to write to you, but I would rather not write with pen and ink;** ¹⁴ **instead I hope to see you soon, and we will talk together face to face.**

15 **Peace to you. The friends send you their greetings. Greet the friends there, each by name.**

The closing of 3 John is very much like that of 2 John and probably represents the elder's habitual style when writing a brief letter. However, verse 15 gives greetings that are different from 2 John, though very similar to what is found in many ordinary Greek letters. This includes the use of the word "friends" (which is the actual Greek word for "friends" here, not the term "brothers" or "brothers and sisters" as elsewhere in the NRSV of 3 John). In fact, curious as it may seem, this typical Greek reference to "friends" is not found in any other New Testament letter (though an exchange of greetings is very commonplace in New Testament letters, as noted in the comments on 2 John 13). Likewise it is rare to find a wish for peace at the end of a letter in the New Testament. Apart from Ephesians 6:23 and 1 Peter 5:14, such wishes are found only in letter *openings* (including 2 John 3). After the tangled church politics of 3 John, and indeed the often intensely combative atmosphere of these letters as a whole, it may be somewhat refreshing to find that the elder's concluding wish for Gaius is for peace.

Works Cited

Carter, Stephen. *The Culture of Disbelief: How American Law and Politics Trivialize Religious Devotion.* New York: Basic Books, 1993.

Merton, Thomas. *New Seeds of Contemplation.* New York: New Directions, 1961.

For Further Reading

Black, C. Clifton. "The First, Second, and Third Letters of John." *The New Interpreter's Bible,* vol. 12, pp. 363–469. Nashville: Abingdon, 1998.

Brown, Raymond E. *The Community of the Beloved Disciple.* New York: Paulist Press, 1979.

———. *The Epistles of John.* AB 30. Garden City, N.Y.: Doubleday, 1982.

Edwards, Ruth B. *The Johannine Epistles.* New Testament Guides. Sheffield, England: Sheffield Academic Press, 1996.

Houlden, J. L. *A Commentary on the Johannine Epistles.* Harper's New Testament Commentaries. San Francisco: Harper & Row, 1973.

Johnson, Thomas F. *1, 2, and 3 John.* New International Biblical Commentary. Peabody, Mass.: Hendrickson, 1993.

Kysar, Robert. *I, II, III John.* Augsburg Commentary on the New Testament. Minneapolis: Augsburg, 1986.

Law, Robert. *The Tests of Life: A Study of the First Epistle of St. John.* 3d ed. Edinburgh: T. & T. Clark, 1914.

Lieu, Judith M. *The Second and Third Epistles of John: History and Background.* Studies of the New Testament and Its World. Edinburgh: T. & T. Clark, 1986.

———. *The Theology of the Johannine Epistles.* New Testament Theology. Cambridge: Cambridge University Press, 1991.

Marshall, I. Howard. *The Epistles of John.* New International Commentary on the New Testament. Grand Rapids: Eerdmans, 1978.

Perkins, Pheme. *The Johannine Epistles.* Revised edition. New Testament
    Message. Wilmington, Del.: Michael Glazier, 1984.

Rensberger, David. *1 John, 2 John, 3 John.* Abingdon New Testament
    Commentaries. Nashville: Abingdon, 1997.

Smalley, Stephen S. *1, 2, 3 John.* Word Biblical Commentary. Waco, Tex.:
    Word, 1984.

Smith, D. Moody. *First, Second, and Third John.* Interpretation. Louisville,
    Ky.: Westminster/John Knox, 1991.

Stott, John R. W. *The Letters of John: An Introduction and Commentary.* 2d
    ed. Tyndale New Testament Commentaries. Grand Rapids: Eerd-
    mans, 1988.

Thompson, Marianne Meye. *1–3 John.* IVP New Testament Commen-
    tary. Downers Grove, Ill.: InterVarsity, 1992.